Rosie's Riveting Recipes

Rosie's Riveting Recipes

WW2 Cooking & Baking

Gayle Martin

Good Oak Press, LLC
Goodoakpress.com

Editor: Cynthia Roedig
Proofreader: Gloria Gray
Cover Photo: Rob Resetar
Cover Design: Good Oak Press, LLC
Typesetting: Good Oak Press, LLC

Acknowledgments

Many thanks to the team who helped me create *Rosie's Riveting Recipes,* including my editor, Cynthia Roedig and my proofreader, Gloria Gray. I couldn't have done this without your help. A big thank you to Rob Resetar for the use of your photo and for your input on the cover design. I would also like to acknowledge two people who are no longer with us, but without whose help this book would not have been possible; my mother, Bee Homes, and my friend, Jim Easterbrook. Both of you are missed.

To Christina

TABLE OF CONTENTS

Author's Preface

In 2000, while I was working a tour docent at the Arizona Historical Society Museum in Tempe, Arizona, I became intrigued with a new exhibit called, *Views from the Home Front.* This gallery chronicled central Arizona's many contributions during World War 2, and it immediately brought to mind all the family stories I'd listened to as a child about what life was like for my parents during the war. It was also while leading tours that I became acquainted with members of the museum's Amazing Arizonans program. These living history interpreters portrayed historic characters from Arizona's past and told the stories of the times they lived in.

It wasn't long before I became inspired to create my own living history character; an average housewife, living in Phoenix 1943, who tells the story of the WW2 Home Front. Thus, *Anna Ferguson, WW2 Housewife & Defense Worker* was born. This composite character represented the countless women across the country who suddenly found themselves facing many unexpected challenges as they fought, "The war back home." Whether it was saving bacon grease, knitting sweaters or gloves for soldiers, or working in defense plants, these women certainly did their part for the war effort and were the unsung heroines who helped lead our nation to victory.

As a motivational speaker and storyteller performing this program, I noticed that much of the audience feedback indicated that people were fascinated by all of the historic artifacts I was presenting, and it was their interest that inspired me to write *Anna's Kitchen: a Compilation of WWII Ration Recipes.* This historic cookbook was published in 2005. It contained historic WW2-era ration recipes, along with stories of home front history. *Anna's Kitchen* received many accolades, but the one I heard the most was, "Wow! This is what my grandmother used to make."

Rosie's Riveting Recipes includes all of the recipes from *Anna's Kitchen,* plus many additional ones, as well as all of the stories of home-front history. It was those everyday WW2-era housewives, our grandmothers and great-grandmothers, who tirelessly coped with food rationing and shortages at home and loved ones fighting abroad, to whom this book is dedicated.

Introduction

Imagine walking into a grocery store and not being allowed to buy whatever you wanted. As hard as this may be to believe, there was a time in our nation's history when this actually happened.

During World War 2, food was rationed in the United States. The country was at war and there was a tremendous fighting force to feed, while at the same time, America's allies in Europe were unable to produce as much food because their farmland had been turned into battlefields. As a means to help cope with the inevitable food shortages at home, and to discourage hoarding, the United States government devised a food rationing program to help ensure that every family would have enough to eat.

A book of food ration stamps had to be obtained for each member of the household. Everyone, from infants to grandparents, had their own ration book. On shopping days, the ration books were taken to the grocery store and the appropriate amount of stamps were redeemed at checkout.

Typically, food ration stamps came in two colors, red and blue. The red stamps were used for meats, cheeses and fats; the blue for canned, bottled, and dried foods. Staples, such as coffee, milk, eggs, butter and sugar were also rationed, as well as chocolate and condiments, such as ketchup. Each ration stamp contained a letter and a number. The number represented the number of ration points each stamp was worth while the letter indicated the ration period, or time frame when the stamps could be redeemed. The scarcer the item, the more ration points were required to purchase the item.

Housewives had to carefully plan their menus, but it wasn't always easy. Each week the average family of four needed about 64 ration points for meats, fats and cheese, and 48 points for processed foods. That came to a little over 100 ration points a week, and if they used up all of their ration points before the end of the ration period, they wouldn't be allowed to purchase any more food until the next ration period began. Food became a scarce commodity, and it simply could not go to waste.

To help ease the burden of food rationing, many families planted Victory Gardens in their yards and home canned their own fruits and vegetables. A new product, called oleo, or margarine, came on the market. Margarine was lower in ration point value and could easily be used in place of butter. It was soft and white and came in a clear cellophane bag. Each bag contained a pearl or bead of yellow food coloring and it was packaged in such a way so as not to confuse or mislead consumers into thinking they were purchasing butter. Many little girls eagerly helped their mothers in the kitchen by breaking the bead and kneading the margarine inside the bag until it turned completely yellow.

Food companies partnered with the government to produce special ration recipe booklets to aid with meal planning. These recipes were designed to help stretch ration points by using different combinations of ingredients or mixing techniques than those used in traditional recipes. Other recipes could be used to create tasty meals from leftovers. These special food ration recipes are presented in the pages that follow. All are historically accurate, and, when appropriate, include suggestions for today's cooks. Most of these recipes are economical, even by today's standards, and many can be prepared in thirty minutes or less. All are delicious.

The early 1940s was a time when the emphasis was on planning wholesome, well-balanced meals and not allowing food go to waste. There was no preoccupation with counting calories, grams of fat, or carbohydrates. What mattered was good nutrition, and it was your patriotic duty to eat nourishing meals in order to stay strong and be able to make your contributions to the war effort.

So now, let's take a trip back in time right in your own kitchen.

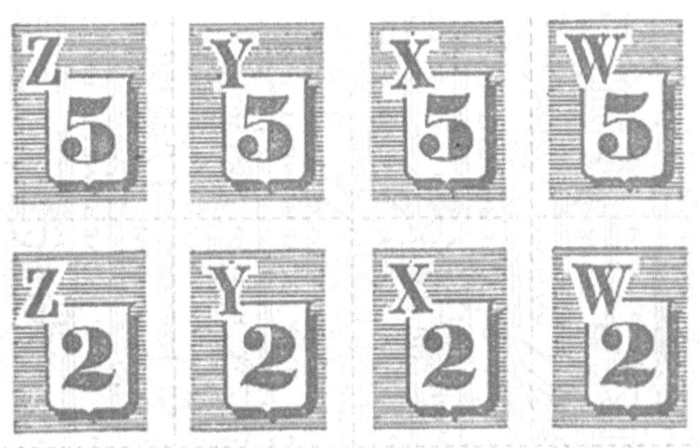

Blue stamps from Ration Book 2. Circa 1943.

20 UNITED STATES OF AMERICA 20
OFFICE OF PRICE ADMINISTRATION

RATION COUPON
FOR
TWENTY
POINTS
PROCESSED FOODS

20 OPA Form R-1325 20

Chapter One

Soups and Stews

20 UNITED STATES OF AMERICA 20
OFFICE OF PRICE ADMINISTRATION

RATION COUPON
FOR
TWENTY
POINTS
MEAT, FATS, FISH, and CHEESES

20 OPA Form R-1415 20

"Food is vital war material. Our fighting forces and those who fight with us need good food. Those who support the fighting forces behind the lines in factory, field, office and home need good food. Every American homemaker who selects food wisely, prepares it cheerfully and conserves it diligently is an important link in our national war effort. In such measures as they guard these links as one of their important war jobs, they are helping to win this war."

— *Your Share: How to Prepare Appetizing, Healthful Meals with Foods Available Today,* Betty Crocker Home Service Staff, 1943

Whether served as an appetizer at the beginning of a meal, or as a meal unto itself, soups and stews were an economical way to help ration points go further, particularly when using "low point" cuts of meat, such as necks or flanks. Some of these recipes use no meat at all.

LUNCHEON SOUP

3 1/2 oz glass or 4-oz cellophane roll dried beef
4 medium potatoes
1 teaspoon salt
3 tablespoons butter
1/4 cup chopped onion
3 cups milk
1/8 teaspoon pepper

Peel potatoes and cut in tiny cubes. Cover with 1 quart boiling water, and salt, and let cook gently until potatoes are tender. Do not drain. Meantime place butter in small saucepan and add chopped onion and beef broken into small pieces. Let cook gently until beef is frizzled and onion clear. Combine with potatoes. Add milk and cook gently for 10 minutes. Add pepper. Serve hot with toasted crackers. Yields 6-8 servings.

Modern adaptation: Use pre-packaged, deli-sliced roast beef. For more zing, add ½ teaspoon season salt and increase pepper to ¼ teaspoon.

CORN CHOWDER WITH BACON

4 strips bacon
4 potatoes
2 cups cream-style corn
2 cups evaporated milk, undiluted
1 onion, chopped
Seasoning of salt and pepper

Cut the potatoes into cubes and cook in 2 cups of boiling salted water until tender. Add the corn and milk. Cut the bacon in small pieces and fry until crisp with the onion. Add to the chowder, season to taste, and serve with crackers. Makes 4 servings.

HAMBURGER VEGETABLE SOUP

3/4 to 1 lb hamburger
1/3 cup chopped onion
2 cups canned or cooked tomatoes
2 cups potato cubes
2 medium, diced carrots
1/3 cup diced celery
2 teaspoons salt
1/4 cup rice
1/8 teaspoon pepper

In a large pot, brown meat and onion lightly in 2 tablespoons fat or drippings. Add the rest of the ingredients along with 1½ quarts water and simmer slowly ¾ to 1 hour. Serve with toast or crackers as the main dish for lunch or supper. Makes 4 servings.

Modern adaptation: To give the soup more zing, use chicken stock instead of water, and add 1 teaspoon cumin. A 14.5 ounce can of tomatoes works nicely. Cooking oil can be used for fat or drippings if using lean ground beef. Additional fat or oil may not be necessary if using regular ground beef.

SOUP MADE FROM VEAL BONES

Make soup from veal bones removed from shoulder roast or breast of veal by cooking slowly for 2 hours in 2 ½ quarts water with seasonings of 1 bay leaf, 4 teaspoons salt, 1 onion, and ½ teaspoon celery salt. Strain and add any desired vegetable, rice, barley or noodles to soup. Makes soup for 4.

Modern adaptation: Most bones—veal, beef, pork, chicken or turkey can be used to make a stock, which can be used to make a soup or used in other recipes. Since many cuts of meat today no longer include the bones, you may need to ask the butcher for a soup bone.

SPLIT PEA SOUP

8 oz cooked cubed ham (about 1 ¼ cups)
1 ham bone
2 ½ quarts ham stock
1 ½ cups split green peas
2 ½ teaspoon salt
¼ teaspoon pepper
½ cup sliced onion
4 tablespoons butter
6 tablespoons flour

Place ham bone, stock, peas, seasonings and onion in large pan. Simmer 2 hours. Melt butter, add flour and blend. Add a small amount of soup stock and stir until smooth, then stir into soup to thicken slightly. Let cubes of ham heat in soup before serving. Makes 4 generous servings.

Modern adaptation: Ham hocks may be used in place of the ham bone. To make a ham stock boil the ham hocks or ham bones in water for approximately one to two hours. Chicken stock can be added to the ham stock or even used as a substitute for the ham stock. Cornstarch can also be used as a thickener instead of the flour.

OYSTER SOUP

1 quart sweet milk*
1 tablespoon corn starch
2 tablespoons margarine
1 slice bacon
1 stalk celery
1 pint oysters
salt and pepper
lemon juice

Put milk into double boiler. Rub together the corn starch and margarine, and stir into hot milk, adding the bacon and celery. Let come to a boil.

Put a few drops of lemon juice over the oysters, and bring them to a boiling point in their own liquid. Drain and (if they should curdle, wash them in a little cold water) turn at once into the milk. Season with salt and pepper, remove the bacon and celery. Pour over broken crackers into a hot tureen or soup plates and serve immediately. Yields 6 servings.

**1940's term for condensed milk*

LAST-MINUTE TOMATO SOUP

1 cup cooked tomatoes
3 cups rich milk*
¾ teaspoon salt
¼ teaspoon pepper
1 tablespoon butter, (if desired)

Stir tomatoes well to break up the pulp and juice. Add milk. Heat, stirring frequently. Add salt and pepper and butter, if desired. Serve immediately. Makes 4 servings.

Modern adaptation: Used canned, diced, Italian-style tomatoes to create a flavorful, elegant soup.

** 1940's term for condensed milk.*

CREAM OF VEGETABLE SOUP

2 tablespoons fat
4 tablespoons flour
¾ teaspoon salt
½ teaspoon pepper
4 cups milk
1 cup cooked vegetable pulp*

Melt fat. Blend in flour, salt and pepper. Stir in milk. Add vegetable pulp. Cook 10 minutes. Makes 6 servings.

** Pureed cooked vegetables (of your choice)*

Modern adaptation: Olive oil may be used instead of "fat." If you do not have a blender or food processor simply chop the vegetables into tiny pieces. Cook over medium heat, stirring frequently, to help keep the milk from scorching. Once soup begins to boil, reduce heat to simmer, stirring occasionally. Cook for 10 minutes, as directed. For more zing, try lemon pepper or season salt instead of salt and pepper.

ONION SOUP

Cook 2 cups finely chopped onions in 2 tablespoons margarine until lightly brown. Sprinkle with 3 tablespoons of flour and stir. Add 1 ½ quarts hot meat broth, made by cooking a soup bone in water, and stir until smooth. Season with salt and pepper and simmer until the onions are tender and flavor well blended. Serve in bowls with a slice of toast in each. Sprinkle grated parmesan cheese on top before serving.

CHICKEN GUMBO

1 chicken
1 onion
1 tablespoon parsley
6 large fresh tomatoes
20 pods okra
1 pod red pepper
3 tablespoons margarine
2 tablespoons flour to thicken
salt and pepper to taste

Cut up chicken. Chop onion and parsley. Skin tomatoes and chop fine, strain off all juice. Slice okra thin. Remove seeds from red pepper and shred. Put margarine into soup kettle, and when hot, add chicken. Cover closely and let simmer for about ten minutes, then add chopped onions, parsley, tomatoes, okra and red pepper, stirring often. When well browned, add juice of tomatoes. Be careful not to let okra scorch as that would spoil the soup. Add three quarts of boiling water. Set back on stove and let simmer gently for an hour. Serve with boiled rice.

Much of the success of this gumbo comes from being highly seasoned –1 sprig thyme or bay leaf and 6 cloves are nice. (Added with vegetables.) Plenty of red pepper – this to the individual taste. Yields 12 to 14 servings.

BEAN SOUP

2 cups cooked beans
1 quart soup stock
1 small stalk celery
1 cup stewed tomatoes
1 tablespoon margarine
salt
paprika

Cook beans and finely divided celery together with soup stock slowly for approximately 20 minutes. Add other ingredients, simmer a few minutes and serve. Yields 6 servings.

Note: "Divided" celery may either by chopped or sliced.

POTATO SOUP

2 cups raw potatoes
2 tablespoons margarine
1 tablespoon chopped onion
1 quart milk
1 ½ teaspoon salt
pepper

Chop potatoes fine or grate them. Add potatoes, margarine, and onion to the milk. Cook the mixture over low heat until the potatoes are tender, stirring regularly. By that time, the starch from the potatoes will have thickened the milk slightly. Add salt and pepper.

Modern Adaptation: As soon as the soup begins to boil cover and simmer on the lowest setting for approximately twenty minutes. Serve with crackers. Top with grated cheddar cheese, and bacon bits if desired.

BEEF STEW

1 to 1 ½ lbs boneless beef (chuck, bottom round, neck, flank or shank)
2 tablespoons flour
4 tablespoons drippings or lard
1 cup chopped onions
4 cloves
1 bay leaf
2 teaspoons salt
1 cup sliced celery
4 small or 3 medium potatoes

Cut meat in 1½-inch pieces. Roll in flour and brown slowly with onion in melted fat for 15 minutes. Add cloves and bay leaf, 1 cup water and half the salt. Cover and simmer for 1 ½ hours. Add vegetables, 1 cup water and rest of salt, cover again and cook another 30 minutes. Thicken gravy if desired. Yields 4 servings.

Modern adaptation: Cooking oil or butter can be used in place of lard or pan drippings, and chicken or beef stock can be added in place of water. If using a prepackaged stock omit the salt. Carrots can also be added.

VEAL STEW WITH CELERY AND NOODLES

2 oz. salt pork
1½ lbs veal breast, or shoulder meat cut in 1½-inch cubes
2 tablespoons flour
2 teaspoons salt
1 cup sliced celery (preferably green celery)
1½ cups noodles

Cut salt pork into tiny pieces and let fry in deep, frying pan or pot roast kettle until crisp and brown. Flour the veal lightly and let pieces brown in the salt pork fat. When well-browned, add salt and 2 cups water and cover tightly. Cook very slowly for 1½ hours. Add celery and continue to cook about 10 minutes or until tender. Thicken gravy if desired. Serve on deep platter around a mound of noodles which have been cooked for about 15-20 minutes in boiling water and drained. Makes 4 servings.

Modern adaptation: Olive oil can be used instead of salt pork. For extra flavor use chicken stock instead of water and omit the salt. If veal is unavailable chicken tenders or beef can be used as a substitute.

SAVORY STEW & DUMPLINGS

2 lb beef, veal or lamb, (cut into 1-inch cubes)
1 bay leaf
2 tablespoons minced parsley
½ cup thyme
salt
pepper
1 cup cut-up carrots
1 cup cut-up turnips
1 cup cut-up celery
1 cup tiny onions
4 cups cubed potatoes
2 tablespoons flour
Bisquick

Roll meat in seasoned flour, brown on all sides in hot drippings. Add a little boiling water. Cover tightly. Simmer 1½ hours. Add remaining ingredients. Thicken liquid for gravy. Drop dumplings, (made from Bisquick) on meat. Cover tightly, cook 15 minutes without lifting cover.

Note: for lamb stew, use less onion, peas in place of turnips.

Modern adaptation: Use 3 to 4 cups of liquid, such as beef or chicken stock or water. Thicken liquid for gravy by making a paste in a prep bowl with 1 or 2 tablespoons flour or cornstarch with 2 or 3 tablespoons of water.

BEEF STEW WITH FEATHER DUMPLINGS

1 lb cubed stewing beef
2 tablespoons fat
¾ cup diced carrots
¾ cup diced turnips
8-10 small white onions
bay leaf
thyme
Worcestershire sauce

Brown 1 pound cubed stewing beef in 2 tablespoons fat. Add 5 cups water and season with salt, pepper, bay leaf, thyme and Worcestershire sauce. Simmer covered, until meat is nearly tender. Add ¾ cup each diced carrots and turnips and 8 to 10 small white onions. (Any desired combinations of vegetables and seasonings may be used.) Cook until vegetables are done.

Thicken stew slightly with flour and water paste. Drop feather dumplings on simmering stew, cover tightly, and simmer 14 minutes. Makes 6 servings.

Feather Dumplings

1 cup sifted flour
1 ¼ teaspoons baking powder
½ teaspoon salt
6 tablespoons milk
2 teaspoons melted fat

Sift flour once, measure, add baking powder and salt, and sift again. Add milk and fat. Then stir quickly and lightly until a very soft dough is formed. Drip by small spoonfuls on simmering stew, making sure each dumpling rests on meat or vegetables. (Dumplings should not settle in liquid. If necessary, pour off excess gravy, returning it to stew after the dumplings are cooked.) Cover kettle tightly and cook gently 14 minutes. Do not remove cover while dumplings cook. Makes 6 to 8 servings.

Note: For the fat, use a little fat skimmed from stew in making these dumplings. It gives extra desired taste.

The four most common gasoline ration couples were A, B, C, and T. All motor vehilces were require to have a windshield sticker with the appropriate letter, and ration coupons to match that letter.

Other WW2 Home Front History — Gasoline Rationing

Gasoline was also rationed during World War 2; however, the reasoning behind it may seem surprising.

The Japanese had captured many of the places in the South Pacific where the United States got rubber for tires, and within days of the attack on Pearl Harbor, the government put a stop on the sale of new tires. In order to make their current tires last longer, restrictions had to placed on how much gasoline Americans could buy. As less gasoline meant less driving, that meant there would be less wear and tear on tires. Some opted to put their cars in their garages and use public transportation until the end of the war. Everyone else had to go to the local War Price and Rationing Board and apply for gasoline ration books.

The four most common classifications for gasoline rationing were A, B, C and T. All motor vehicles were required to have a sticker on the windshield with the appropriate letter and only use ration coupons with the same letter. A stickers, the most common, were considered non-essential, and those who had them were allowed to purchase up to four gallons of gasoline a week. B stickers were for carpools, and C stickers were designated for commercial use. Red Cross workers, doctors, hospital staff, and members of the clergy were among those considered essential enough to qualify for C coupons. Those drivers who qualified for B or C coupons could buy as much gas as they needed, but were encouraged to conserve nonetheless. T coupons were for trucks, and were limited to five gallons of gasoline each week. To help discourage the use of black market coupons, license plate numbers had to be written on each coupon, and the gasoline attendant checked to be sure the license number on the coupon matched the number on the car.

"Is this trip necessary?"

— United States government public service slogan
to help discourage driving.

20 UNITED STATES OF AMERICA 20
OFFICE OF PRICE ADMINISTRATION

RATION COUPON
FOR
TWENTY
POINTS
MEAT, FATS, FISH, and CHEESES

20 OPA Form R-1615 20

CHAPTER TWO

BEEF, VEAL AND LAMB

20 UNITED STATES OF AMERICA 20
OFFICE OF PRICE ADMINISTRATION

RATION COUPON
FOR
TWENTY
POINTS
MEAT, FATS, FISH, and CHEESES

20 OPA Form R-1615 20

"In spite of the heavy demands on America's supply of meat because of the war, our share at home will be enough – if we use it wisely, learn to extend it with other foods – and make the most of every bit available."

— *Your Share: How to Prepare Appetizing, Healthful Meals with Foods Available Today,* Betty Crocker Home Service Staff, 1943

During the war, meat became a precious and tightly rationed commodity. Certain cuts of beef, such as steaks, virtually disappeared from the market. There were times when even ground beef was hard to come by. The ration point cost of meats was usually lowest on those cuts with large amounts of fat and bone, and even the least desirable cuts could be stretched. The bone could be boiled and used as soup stock with the excess fat removed and rendered, or melted down into lard for use in baking. So scarce did meats and fats become that even small pieces of lard left on food wrappers would be steamed down and reused. Once the rendered fats were no longer suitable for cooking or baking they would be placed in a tin can and taken back to the butcher to be used for explosives and ammunition. Nothing ever went to waste.

Today's cooks, however, may discover that veal is difficult to find. Many supermarkets simply no longer carry it, and those that do may have a limited selection or the prices may be exceedingly high. However, boneless chicken breasts, can often be used in many recipes in place of veal.

BROWNED ROAST BEEF HASH WITH GRILLED TOMATOES

3 tablespoons butter or meat drippings
2 cups chopped cooked beef
2 cups chopped cooked potatoes
1/4 cup chopped onion
1/2 teaspoon salt
1/8 teaspoon pepper
2 large tomatoes

Melt butter in a hot frying pan. Spread the well-mixed ingredients evenly over bottom of pan. Cook slowly and stir until browned. Serve on a hot platter with half tomatoes that have been dotted with butter and grilled under the broiler until browned. Yields 4-5 servings.

BEEF AND OATMEAL LOAF

1 ¼ lbs ground beef chuck
¼ lb ground pork
¼ cup minced onion
1 cup uncooked oatmeal
2 ¼ teaspoons salt
¼ teaspoon pepper
1 teaspoon dry mustard
¼ cup catsup
1 egg, slightly beaten
1 cup water

Mix the meat, onions and dry ingredients. To this mixture add catsup, egg and water. Place in loaf pan and bake for 1 hour and 15 minutes at 325°F. Makes 8 servings.

BEEF BISCUIT ROLL

1 lb ground beef
1/2 cup chopped onion
1/2 cup chopped green pepper
2 tablespoons butter or bacon drippings
1/3 cup milk
2 cups flour
2 - 3 teaspoons baking powder
1/2 teaspoon salt
1/8 teaspoon pepper

Brown the beef, onion and green pepper in butter or drippings in a frying pan. Add seasonings.

Make biscuit dough by sifting flour, salt, baking powder, cutting in bacon drippings, add milk slowly until the dry ingredients are moist. Roll out on a floured board to about ¼-inch thickness. Brush with melted drippings or melted butter. Spread with meat mixture and roll like a jelly roll. If dough is too soft, chill in refrigerator first, then cut in 1½-inch slices. Place in greased pan, cut side up, brush tops with melted butter or beef drippings. Bake 20-25 minutes at 450° F. Serve with brown gravy or cheese sauce. Makes 5-6 servings.

Modern adaptation: As today's baking powders are double-acting, limit baking powder to 1½ to 2 teaspoons. Brush the dough with olive oil. While meat is baking add 1 to 2 tablespoons of flour to the pan drippings. Add milk and heat to simmering to make a gravy, or top with your favorite hamburger condiments.

FLUFFY MEAT LOAF

1 lb ground beef or veal
½ lb ground pork
2 cups bread crumbs
1 egg, beaten
1½ cups milk
4 tablespoons chopped onion
¼ teaspoon dry mustard
½ teaspoon sage
2 teaspoons salt
¼ teaspoon pepper

Mix ingredients thoroughly. Pack into greased 4 x 8-inch loaf pan. Bake 1½ hours at 350°F.

Variations

For Beef Loaf: Use 1 tablespoon horseradish and 1 tablespoon catsup in place of mustard and sage.

For catsup-topped* loaf: spread 3 tablespoons catsup over top before baking.

* *Catsup is a varient of the word ketchup.*

BEEF SCALLOPINI

¾ lb bottom round steak
2 tablespoons flour
¼ cup chopped onions
2 tablespoons butter, margarine or pan drippings
½ cup evaporated milk diluted with ½ cup water
1½ teaspoon salt
2 cups coarsely crushed corn flakes
¼ cup melted butter

Cut round steak in ½-inch cubes and dust with flour. Brown onion and meat in fat. Add evaporated milk gradually and stir until thick. Add salt. Cover and let simmer on a low heat for ½ hour until tender. Cover the bottom of a baking dish with crushed corn flakes, add a layer of meat and gravy, repeat, alternating layers ending with crumbs on top. Pour melted butter over top and bake in 350° F oven for 30 minutes. Yields 4 servings.

Modern adaptation: For a little more zing, add 2 teaspoons Worcestershire sauce along or red cooking wine with the salt.

BARBECUED BEEF LOAVES

1 1/2 lbs ground beef
1/2 lb ground lean pork
1/2 cup fine, dry bread crumbs
1/2 cup evaporated milk
2 teaspoons salt
1/8 teaspoon pepper
2 tablespoons chopped onion

Mix bread crumbs, milk and seasonings. Add meats and onion and blend well. Shape into 8 individual oblong meat loaves and place in shallow pan.

Make barbecue sauce by heating together ½ cup catsup, 1/3 cup vinegar, 1 tablespoon Worcestershire sauce, 1 teaspoon chili powder and 2 tablespoons chopped onion. Pour over the loaves and bake 45 minutes at 350° F, basting once or twice. Makes 8 servings.

Modern adaptation: For more flavorful loaves, try using 1 pound ground beef and 1 pound ground pork or pork sausage, and add other seasonings, such as onion powder, garlic powder, or steak seasoning blends. Make loaves approximately one-inch thick to form rectangular-shaped patties. Use sourdough or Kaiser rolls to serve loaves as sandwiches.

CREAMED DRIED BEEF ON BAKED POTATOES

¼ lb dried, beef broken in small pieces
¼ cup butter
¼ cup chopped onions
¼ cup flour
1 cup evaporated milk diluted with 1 cup water
¼ cup green pepper
1 teaspoon Worcestershire sauce
2 – 4 baked potatoes, split open

Brown onions in butter and blend in flour. Add milk gradually and stir until thick. Add remaining ingredients and serve over split, baked potatoes. Yield: 4 servings.

Modern adaptation: Pre-packaged, deli-sliced roast beef can be used as a substitute for dried beef. Try over toast or biscuits.

BEEF POTATO BURGERS

¾ lb ground beef or chuck
¼ lb ground pork
1½ cups coarsely grated raw potatoes
½ cup coarsely grated onion
¼ cup chopped green pepper
1½ teaspoon salt
¼ teaspoon pepper
2 tablespoons butter, margarine or drippings

Combine ground meat, potatoes, onions, green pepper and seasonings and shape into 6 flat patties. Fry patties in butter or fat until brown. Makes 6 servings

HUNGARIAN GOULASH

2 lbs beef chuck, neck or flank meat
2 tablespoons butter, margarine or drippings
1 cup chopped onion
1 cup water
1/8 teaspoon caraway seed (if desired)
1/2 teaspoon marjoram
1 1/2 teaspoon salt
1 clove garlic
paprika

Cut meat into 1-inch cubes. Let onion brown in butter, then add meat and let it brown lightly. Add caraway seed, marjoram, salt, chopped garlic and enough paprika to create a noticeable red color. Add 1 cup water, cover and simmer for 2 ½ hours. Add more water if necessary. Whole potatoes may be added to the goulash ½ hour before done. Some goulash recipes call for the addition of tomatoes. Strained tomatoes may be substituted for water in this recipe. Makes 6 servings.

Note: Serve over noodles or your favorite pasta.

BRAISED SHORT RIBS OR BEEF WITH VEGETABLES

2 lbs beef short ribs
3 tablespoons flour
2 tablespoons lard
2 teaspoons salt
1/8 teaspoon pepper
1/2 onion
2 carrots
1/2 green pepper (if desired)
1/2 cup celery
1/2 cup water

Cut short ribs into individual squares and flour them. Brown slowly on all sides in lard, approximately 20-30 minutes. Add seasonings, minced onion, and water. Cover tightly and simmer for 2 hours. Add vegetables, cut small and continue cooking 30-40 minutes. Remove meat and place on serving platter. Thicken vegetable gravy with 1 tablespoon flour stirred into ½ cup water. Makes 5 servings.

Modern adaptation: Use butter or cooking oil instead of lard and dry red wine instead of water. Decrease salt to one teaspoon.

CROWN ROAST OF BACK RIBS

1 1/2 lbs. back ribs
1 teaspoon salt
1/2 cup chopped onion
3 tablespoons butter
3 cups soft bread crumbs
1 teaspoon salt
1/8 teaspoon pepper
1 teaspoon poultry seasonings

Rub back ribs with salt. Mix remaining ingredients to form dressing. Sew ends of ribs together to resemble a crown. Place stuffing inside of ribs and bake in 350° F oven for 2-3 hours or until tender. Makes 4 servings.

Modern adaptation: Ribs can be tacked together with wooden toothpicks or toothpicks or skewers. (Do not use plastic.) After cooking, allow the ribs to rest before removing the toothpicks. Three pieces of bread, with crusts removed, and cut into cubes, can also be used to make the dressing. You can also try adding chopped celery, nuts, or mushrooms.

BOILED BEEF DINNER

3 ½ lbs cross cut fore shank
1 ½ tablespoons salt
4 potatoes
4 medium-sized onions
4 large carrots

Place shanks and salt in stew kettle and cover with water. Cover and simmer slowly for 1½ hours, or until tender. Add vegetables and continue cooking for about ½ hour or until vegetables are tender. Serve a horseradish sauce with meat. Makes 4 servings.

For sauce: Make 1 cup of medium-thick white sauce* and stir in ¼ cup prepared horseradish. A pre-packaged horseradish sauce may be used as a substitute.

** To make white sauce melt 2 tablespoons of butter in a saucepan over medium heat. Add 2 tablespoons of flour and still until well combined. Pour in 2 cups of milk, stirring constantly until sauce thickens. Add more milk if a thinner sauce is desired.*

POT-LUCK PIE

½ cup chopped onions
2 tablespoons chopped green peppers (optional)
2 tablespoons fat or drippings
2 cups (1 lb) cooked cubed beef
1 cup sliced carrots, cooked
2 cups canned peas, well drained
1 cup whole-kernel corn, well drained
6 tablespoons fat or drippings
5 tablespoons enriched flour
1 cup milk
1½ cups vegetable liquid, beef broth, or water
1½ teaspoon salt
½ teaspoon pepper
½ teaspoon Worcestershire sauce (optional)

Pan-fry onion and green peppers in fat until tender. Remove from fat. Add to combined meat, carrots, peas and corn. Melt 6 tablespoons fat in frying pan; add flour; mix well. Add liquids gradually; cook until thick and smooth, stirring constantly. Add seasonings, meat, and vegetables to mixture. Allow to simmer until vegetables are heated. Turn into 2-quart casserole. Top with the following:

1½ cups sifted enriched flour
1½ teaspoons baking powder
¼ teaspoon salt
3 tablespoons shortening
¼ cup chopped olives (optional)
9 tablespoons milk, about

Sift flour, measure, add baking powder and salt and sift again. Cut in shortening until mixture resembles course meal. Add olives, mix well. Add milk; stir until all flour is dampened.

Rollout on lightly floured board to about ½-inch thickness. Cut with diamond-shaped cutter. Place over hot mixture. Bake in 375°F oven until biscuits are done. Garnish with parsley. Serve immediately. Serves 6.

Modern adaptation: To help make preparing this dish a little simpler cook the onion and cubed beef together in a saucepan while steaming any vegetables that need to be cooked in a vegetable steamer or in the microwave. Canned vegetables can also be used. Butter, cooking oil, or a combination thereof can be used for the 6 tablespoons of fat or drippings. Place fat in a large frying pan and add flour, liquids, seasonings, meat and vegetables as instructed in the recipe.

Today, most baking powders are double-acting. Cut baking powder to 1 teaspoon. If you don't have a cookie cutter use a glass to cut biscuits. Bake in a 375° F oven for 25 to 35 minutes or until the sauce is bubbling and the biscuits have turned a light golden brown.

HALF-HOUR DINNER

1 pound ground raw meat
$^2/_3$ cup quick oats
1 teaspoon salt
2 cups water
1 teaspoon grated onion
margarine
vegetables
$1^1/_2$ cups enriched all-purpose flour
1 teaspoon salt
$2\ ^1/_2$ teaspoons baking powder
$^1/_2$ cup quick oats
1 cup milk

Mix meat with $^2/_3$ cup oats, salt and ½ cup water. Season with onion, mix well. Form into 24 small balls. Brown in margarine. Add equal quantity of desired vegetables and remaining (1½ cups) water. Cover and cook. Sift and measure flour. Re-sift with salt and baking powder. Stir in ½ cup quick oats. Measure, add milk and mix lightly. Drop by heaping teaspoons onto steaming vegetables and meat. Cook covered for 20 minutes. Makes 8 – 10 dumplings.

STUFFED HAMBURGER ON ONION SLICES

1 pound hamburger
1 tablespoon melted margarine
1 tablespoon catsup*
4 slices bread
1 egg beaten
1 tablespoon milk

Divide hamburger into six equal servings. Roll or pat out as thin as possible, sprinkle with salt and pepper. Make dressing by combining bread, milk, and catsup with 1 tablespoon melted margarine. Place a spoonful of dressing on each square. Bring edges of meat up over the dressing and pat into shape, being sure all dressing is covered. Fry in hot margarine in skillet. When brown on both sides, add ½ cup water, cover and cook over low hear 8 to 10 minutes. Serve on raw onion slices.

**Catsup is a variation of the word ketchup.*

EMERGENCY STEAK

1 lb ground beef or hamburger
½ cup milk
1 cup Wheaties
1 teaspoon salt
¼ teaspoon pepper
1 tablespoon chopped onion

Mix all ingredients thoroughly. Place on pan, pat into T-bone steak shape, 1-inch thick. Broil 8 to 15 minutes at 500º. Turn once. Serves 6.

SIX-LAYER DINNER

2 cups sliced raw potatoes
2 cups cooked celery
2 cups ground beef
1 cup sliced raw onions, (or less, if desired)
1 cup finely cut green pepper, (or less, if desired)
2 cups cooked tomatoes
2 teaspoons salt
¼ teaspoon pepper

Place potatoes, celery, ground beef, onions, green pepper and tomatoes in layers in greased 8 x 12-inch baking dish. Season layers with salt and pepper. Garnish with green pepper slices. Bake about 2 hours at 350° F. Serves 6.

BEEF AND POTATO PUFF

2 tablespoons chopped onion
2 tablespoons chopped parsley
2 tablespoons margarine
3 cups ground cooked beef
3 cups mashed potatoes
1 cup gravy or milk
salt and pepper
3 eggs

Cook the onion and parsley for a few minutes in the margarine. Add the meat, potatoes, and gravy or milk and mix thoroughly. Season to taste. Add beaten egg yolks, then fold in the egg whites. Pile lightly into a greased baking dish and bake at 350° F for 1 hour or until set in the center and lightly browned. Serve in the dish. Top with tomato sauce, if desired. Yields 6 servings.

MEATBALL PANCAKES

3 eggs, separated
½ lb ground beef
¼ teaspoon baking powder
½ teaspoon salt
dash of pepper
1 teaspoon lemon juice
1 tablespoon minced parsley
1 tablespoon grated onion

Beat egg yolks until light. Blend in ground beef, baking powder, salt and pepper, lemon juice, parsley and onions. Fold in stiffly beaten egg whites. Drop spoonfuls on hot greased griddle. When puffed and brown, turn and brown on other side. Serve immediately with a mushroom sauce, if desired. Or choose a creamed vegetable or potatoes to go with the pancakes. Serves 6.

CURRY OF MEAT

1 onion, sliced
3 tablespoons margarine
3 pints sliced tart apples or green tomatoes
3 cups chopped cooked meat (beef, pork, lamb or veal)
meat broth or gravy
curry powder
salt

Cook the onion in the margarine. Add the apples or green tomatoes, cover and cook until tender. Add the meat (beef, pork, lamb or veal) and heat thoroughly. If the mixture is too thick, thin it slightly with meat broth, gravy, or water. Season to taste with curry powder and salt. Serve with rice or noodles. Yields 6 servings.

RAINBOW CASSEROLE

One red, one green and one yellow vegetable (fresh or canned)
2 potatoes
1 onion
salt and pepper
1 tablespoon margin, melted
1/2 pound ground beef
1/2 teaspoon salt
1/3 cup quick oats
1/4 cup cold water

Arrange vegetables in layers in a well-greased, 9-inch casserole. Top with sliced potatoes and onion. Season with salt and pepper, dot with margarine. Pour water or juice from the cans over the vegetables.

Meat Crust Topping: Combine meat, salt, oats and water. Mix well with fork. Pat into circle. Cut vent in center and cut into 6 or 8 wedges, place on top of vegetables. Brush with melted margarine. Bake at 375°F for 30 – 35 minutes, serve hot. Yields: 4 to 6 servings.

PANNED CABBAGE AND CORNED BEEF

3 tablespoons margarine
2 -3 quarts shredded cabbage
2 cups cooked corned beef, in small pieces
vinegar
salt and pepper

Heat margarine in a large pan, add shredded cabbage, cover to keep in the steam, and cook for 10 to 15 minutes, stirring thoroughly. Add corned beef, cut into small pieces, and heat until piping hot. Season to taste with salt, pepper and a little vinegar. Yields 6 servings.

TOASTWICHES

½ lb ground beef or hamburger
½ cup milk
1 tablespoon minced onion
½ teaspoon salt
½ teaspoon pepper
4 slices of bread, toasted on one side
butter
prepared mustard*
bacon fat**

Mix ground beef, milk, onion, salt and pepper. Spread the untoasted side of bread with butter and prepared mustard. Spread with meat mixture. Dot with a little bacon fat. Broil about 7 minutes. Serves 4.

** Prepared mustard is a mixture of dry mustard mixed with water, vinegar, wine or beer. Store bought mustards would also be suitable for this recipe.*

*** Bacon fat is another term for bacon grease, which, at that time, was a popular cooking fat. Butter or margarine may be used as a substitute for bacon grease.*

STUFFED BONED SHOULDER OF VEAL*

1 square cut veal shoulder – boned for stuffing, (5-6 lbs)

Dressing

½ cup chopped onion
½ cup chopped celery
½ chopped green pepper
2 teaspoons salt
½ teaspoon poultry seasoning
2 cups soft bread crumbs
¼ cup melted butter, margarine or drippings
1 tablespoon lemon juice, if desired

Mix onion, celery, peppers, seasoning, bread and add melted fat and lemon. Place on inside of veal shoulder, and close the 2 open sides by sewing or with skewers laced together with a cord. Place on rack in open pan, rub with 2 teaspoons salt. Roast in 300-325° F oven for 32 minutes per pound. Serve with border of crabapple pickles and parsley or watercress. Yields 3 servings to the pound.

** Due to the decline in demand for veal in recent years, veal shoulder may no longer be available. This recipe has been included for historical discussion purposes.*

VEAL SHORTCAKE

1 cup cubed leftover veal roast
1½ tablespoons flour
1 tablespoon minced onion
½ cup diced celery
1 tablespoon butter
1 cup milk
½ teaspoon salt
½ teaspoon Worcestershire sauce

Cube veal, roll in flour and brown lightly with onion and celery in butter. Add milk slowly, stir until smooth and thickened. Season with salt and Worcestershire sauce and serve between halves of split, buttered biscuits. Yields 4 servings.

VEAL LOAF

1 lb ground veal shoulder or breast meat
1/4 lb ground pork shoulder
1/3 cup cracker crumbs
1 1/2 teaspoon salt
1/4 teaspoon pepper
1 egg
1/3 cup evaporated milk
2 teaspoons lemon juice
1/2 teaspoon celery salt (if desired)

Mix all ingredients and pack into oiled loaf pan. Bake at 350° F oven for 1½ hours. Makes 6 servings.

Note: Ground turkey or chicken may be used in place of veal.

VEAL AND RICE CASSEROLE

2 cups cooked veal, cubed
1/4 cup raw rice
3 tablespoons butter
3 tablespoons flour
1 1/2 cups milk
1 1/2 teaspoon salt
1/8 teaspoon pepper
3 tablespoons chopped green pepper
3 tablespoons chopped pimiento
1/4 cup chopped green olives
1/4 cups chopped celery

Cut veal into small cubes. Cook rice in boiling salt water for 20 minutes. Drain and rinse. Make a sauce by melting butter, adding flour and stirring in milk. When thickened, season and add green pepper, pimiento, olives, and celery. Add veal. Put layers of rice and veal mixture alternately in a baking dish, finishing with a layer of rice. Dot with bits of butter and bake at 350° F for 45 minutes. Makes 5 servings.

MAKING THE MOST OF A LEG OF LAMB

Lamb legs weigh from 4 to 7 lbs. If you do not have sufficient points to purchase a whole leg, the dealer may be willing to cut it in half for you. If you purchase the full leg, have 3 or 4 sirloin steaks cut from the heavy end of the leg first. Broil these for one meal and roast the remainder for the following day. Use leftover lamb in curry, patties, lamb pie or other casserole dish.

To roast lamb, place fat side up on rack in open roasting pan. Insert small slivers of garlic near the bone if desired. Rub with salt and pepper and roast in 325°F oven for 35 to 40 minutes to the pound or until the meat thermometer registers 180° F (well-done for lamb). Make gravy from drippings.

— *69 Ration Recipes for Meat from Marie Gifford's Kitchen*, published by Armour and Company, Chicago, circa 1942.

BRAISED LAMB SHANKS

4 lamb shanks
4 tablespoons fat
1 teaspoon salt
¼ teaspoon pepper
2 cups water
1 cup cut-up carrots
1 cup cut-up potatoes
½ cup cut-up celery
½ cup cup-up onion

Brown lamb shanks in fat. Add salt and pepper and water. Simmer covered 1½ hours or bake in moderate oven (350° F). Add more water if necessary. Add carrots, potatoes, celery and onion. Continue cooking until tender (30 minutes to 1 hour). Thicken juice with small amounts of flour before serving. Serves 4.

BARBECUED LAMB SHANKS

3 lamb shanks (about 3 lbs)
1 tablespoon lard

Sauce

1 cup chopped onions
½ teaspoon pepper
2 teaspoons sugar
1 teaspoon mustard (dry)
1 teaspoon paprika
4 teaspoons Worcestershire sauce
½ teaspoon Tabasco sauce
½ cup catsup
¼ cup vinegar
½ cup water

Melt fat in heavy frying pan and brown lamb shanks. Combine ingredients for sauce and pour over shanks. Cover and bake at 350° F for 2 hours or until tender. Yields 4-5 servings.

BRAISED LAMB SHOULDER CHOPS AND GRAVY

4-5 shoulder lamb chops cut ½-inch thick
2 tablespoons butter, margarine or drippings
2 tablespoons flour
1 tablespoon Worcestershire sauce
1½ teaspoon salt
pepper
1 cup milk

Brown the chops slowly in the hot fat. When they are well browned remove from pan. Stir the flour, salt and pepper into the fat and cook until flour is brown. Add milk and Worcestershire sauce and stir until thick. Place meat back in gravy, cover and simmer over very low heat for 35 minutes. Makes 4-5 servings.

SNOWY LOAF

2 lbs ground lamb shoulder
2 teaspoons salt
¼ clove garlic, minced very fine
½ cup evaporated milk
½ cup fine cracker crumbs
1 egg
3 cups mashed potatoes

Combine the lamb, salt, garlic, milk, egg and cracker crumbs. Pack in pan and bake for 1 hour and 20 minutes in a 325° F oven. This is best baked in an oiled bread tin, for the loaf then has a good shape. When the loaf is baked, turn out of the pan and frost with the hot mashed potatoes. A pastry tube may be used to ruffle the mashed potatoes over the top. Place in a 400° F oven long enough to brown the potatoes (about 10 min.). Makes 6-7 servings.

LAMB AND VEGETABLE PIE

1 1/2 lbs stewing lamb (about 2 cups cubed, lean meat)
1 quart water
1 teaspoon salt
1 or 2 bay leaves
Few peppercorns
1 cup sliced onions
1/2cup chopped celery
1 1/2 cups cubed rutabagas* or turnips
1 1/2 cups sliced carrots
1 cup string beans or cubed parsnips
5 tablespoons enriched flour
3 tablespoons fat or drippings
2 teaspoon salt
1/8 teaspoon pepper
1/2 teaspoon thyme
1 cup lamb stock
1 cup tomatoes, juice and pulp

Remove and discard fat, bone and tough skin from meat. Place in heavy kettle or deep cooker. Add water, salt, bay leaves, and peppercorns. Cover and allow to simmer slowly until meat is partially tender (about 1 hour). Remove bay leaves and peppercorns. Add vegetables. Cook slowly until vegetables are partially tender. Add water, if needed. Drain thoroughly, reserving liquid for gravy. Turn meat and vegetables into large casserole. Combine flour, fat, seasonings to make smooth paste. Add 1 cup reserved lamb stock and tomatoes gradually; mix well. Cook over direct heat, stirring constantly until thick and smooth. Pour over vegetable-meat mixture.

Continued on next page...

Top with the following:

Pastry

1½ cups sifted flour
¾ teaspoon baking powder (optional)
1 teaspoon salt
½ cup shortening
5 to 6 tablespoons cold water

Sift flour once, measure. Add baking powder and salt; sift again. Cut in shortening to about the size of small peas. Add water, a little at a time, until dough is moist enough to hold together. Chill. Roll out on lightly floured board in a circle about 1/8-inch thick. From center of dough, cut a 3-to-4-inch circle. Place larger circle of pastry over casserole. Trim, flute, and fasten to edge of casserole. With remaining pastry, cut out small stars, circles, or triangles, arrange attractively on surface of pastry. Bake in hot oven, (425° F) for 20 minutes or until done. Serves 6.

Note: Beef, veal, or pork may be substituted for lamb; omit thyme. If using canned beans, add a few minutes before removing mixture from heat.

** Rutabagas is an old term for turnips*

LAMB CURRY

1½ cups cubed cold lamb
2 tablespoons butter or margarine
¾ cup chopped onion
¼ cup green pepper (if desired)
½ cup chopped celery
1 clove garlic
1 teaspoon curry powder
1½ teaspoon salt
1 tablespoon Worcestershire sauce
2 cups stock – made from lamb bones
2 tablespoons flour

Brown onions, pepper, celery and garlic in the fat. Add the meat, curry powder, salt and Worcestershire sauce and stock. Cook for about 30 minutes over a low heat. Thicken with the flour mixed with ¼ cup cold water. Serve in a ring of boiled rice. Makes 4 servings.

DEVILED LAMB NECK SLICES

1½ lbs lamb neck slices (cut ¾-inch thick)
2 tablespoons butter
1 cup sliced onion
1 tablespoon vinegar
½ teaspoon dry mustard

Brown lamb neck slices and onion in butter in a heavy skillet over low heat about 20 minutes. Add seasonings and 2 cups water, cover tightly and simmer about 1½ hours. Thicken gravy with 2 tablespoons flour blended with ¼ cold water if desired. Serve on a bed of mashed potatoes. Makes 4 servings.

GRILLED LAMB PATTIES WITH PEARS

2 lbs ground lamb shoulder meat
1½ teaspoon salt
¼ teaspoon pepper
¼ cup dry bread crumbs
¼ cup undiluted evaporated milk
6 strips bacon
1 No. 2 ½ can pears*
¼ cup mayonnaise

Season lamb, add milk and crumbs and shape lightly into 6 patties. Wrap each with a strip of bacon, skewered in place with a toothpick. Place on preheated broiler rack 3½ inches under heat unit. Broil 5 minutes, then turn. Add pears to rack with a teaspoon of mayonnaise in center of each. Finish broiling an additional 6-7 minutes. Yields 6 servings.

** 3 ½ cups or 29 ounces*

LAMB PIE – POTATO PUFF CRUST

1½ lbs lamb (breast or shoulder) cut in 1½-inch pieces
2 tablespoons lard or meat drippings
2½ teaspoons salt
¼ teaspoon pepper
4 carrots, sliced
1 cup green lima beans
4 small onions
2 cups mashed potatoes

Flour lamb pieces lightly. Using heavy stew kettle or deep frying pan, brown meat lightly on all sides in lard or drippings for 15 minutes. Add 3 cups water and seasonings. Cover tightly and simmer for 1½ hours. Add carrots, lima beans and onions and continue to cook until tender. Transfer to casserole, top with wreath of fluffy mashed potatoes. Place under broiler just long enough to brown the potatoes. Yield: 4 servings.

Other WW2 Home Front History — Shoe Rationing

Like beef, leather was hard to come by during the war years. It was needed to make boots and other products for our fighting forces, so civilian consumers had to make do with less. Rubber was also in short supply. It too was needed to make shoes and boots. Most people were limited to three new pairs of shoes a year, which was undoubtedly challenging to families with growing children. Families and neighbors would have had to share their resources by providing hand-me-down shoes for children. In some instances, un-rationed shoes, made out of cardboard, were available.

"I remember when I was a teenager I wore un-rationed sandals made out of cardboard. They weren't bad. In fact, I kind of liked them."

— Bee Homes

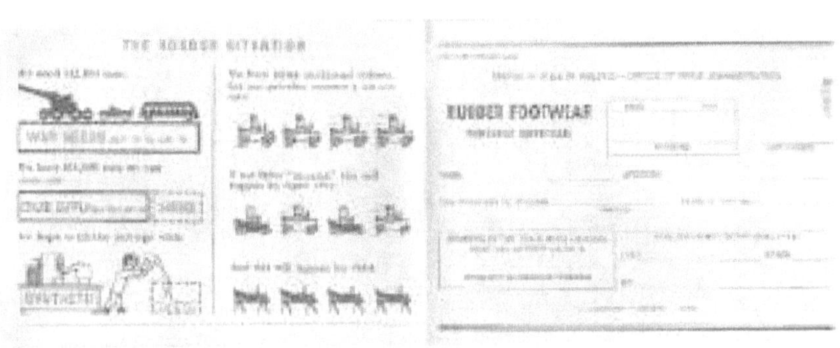

Purchase certificate for a new pair of rubber shoes. Circa 1942. To buy a pair of rubber shoes your first had to apply at your rationing board. If your appliation was approved you had to turn in your old shoes, and only work shoes could be purchased.

20 UNITED STATES OF AMERICA 20
OFFICE OF PRICE ADMINISTRATION

RATION COUPON
FOR
TWENTY
POINTS
PROCESSED FOODS

20 OPA Form R-1325 20

CHAPTER THREE

Ham and Pork

20 UNITED STATES OF AMERICA 20
OFFICE OF PRICE ADMINISTRATION

RATION COUPON
FOR
TWENTY
POINTS
MEAT, FATS, FISH, and CHEESES

20 OPA Form R-1615 20

MAKING THE MOST OF A HAM SHANK

If points allow, buy a ham shank weighing about 5 lbs. Cook it whole in water to cover; use part of the meat for a "boiled" ham and vegetable dinner, the extra meat for a leftover ham dish, and the broth and bone for split pea soup.

Some dealers will split a shank lengthwise, allowing smaller purchases. In this case, the meaty, boneless half may be used for slicing and frying, or cooking in water. The bony side may be used for soup and dishes made from leftover cooked ham.

For "Boiled" Ham Dinner, simmer the shank in water to cover for 2 hours. Add any desired vegetables during the last 30 minutes of cooking.

— *69 Ration Recipes for Meat from Marie Gifford's Kitchen,* Armour and Company, Chicago, circa 1943.

Just like beef and lamb, ham and pork were also rationed. Meats were not only rationed for the consumer, they were rationed for grocery stores and butcher shops as well. Grocers, who collected ration stamps from their customers, kept those used ration stamps in order to restock their supplies. The ration boards would exchange the used ration stamps for certificates that would allow the grocers to buy the products they needed for their shops, and the amount of meat products they could purchase was in direct proportion to what they had sold to their customers.

HAM LOAF

1 lb ground smoked ham
1 lb ground pork
3 cups Wheaties
2 eggs, well beaten
1 cup milk
1 teaspoon salt
½ teaspoon pepper

Mix all ingredients thoroughly. Pack into greased loaf pan (4x8 inches). Bake 1½ hours in moderate oven (350° F).

Variations

For Peanut Ham Loaf: Add 4 tablespoons peanut butter to other ingredients.

Festive Ham Loaf: Bake in ring mold. Garnish with hot fruits (pineapple or cinnamon apple slices, peach halves, etc.)

Modern adaptation: If ground ham is not available ground beef or ground chicken may be used as substitutes.

JELLIED HAM LOAF

2½ lb ham shank
1 tablespoon gelatin
¼ cup cold water
2 bouillon cubes
2 tablespoons horseradish
2 tablespoons prepared mustard
1½ cups Wheaties

Cover ham shank with water. Boil. Simmer for 2 hours. Take meat from bone and grind enough for 2 cups. Save 2 cups of water for ham stock. Soften gelatin in cold water. Dissolve bouillon cubes in ham stock. Add cooked ham, horseradish, mustard and Wheaties. Chill until firm in oiled bread loaf pan, (4 x 8 inches). Unmold and slice. Serves 8 –10.

HAM AND CHEESE SPOON LOAF

2 cups grated cooked ham (about 12 oz)
3 tablespoons butter
2 tablespoons chopped onion
3 tablespoons flour
½ teaspoon paprika
1 cup evaporated milk diluted with 1 cup water
12 soda crackers
1 cup ground American cheese
4 eggs, separated

Cook chopped onion in melted butter. Blend in flour and paprika. Add milk gradually, and stir until thick. Put ham, cheese and soda cracker through food chopper and combine with sauce. Add beaten egg yolk. Fold in stiffly beaten egg whites. Bake in buttered baking dish in low oven 275 - 300° F for 45 minutes. Makes 4-6 servings.

HAM AND EGG PIE

2 cups cubed, cooked ham
3 tablespoons butter or margarine
¼ cup chopped celery
¼ cup chopped onion
4 tablespoons flour
2 cups milk
1¼ teaspoon salt
4 hard-cooked eggs

Let onion and celery cook until clear in butter, then stir in flour and milk and stir until thickened. Season and add eggs cut into quarters and the cubed ham. Place in a baking dish and cover with top crust made thus:

Crust: Sift 1 cup flour, measure and resift with ½ teaspoon salt and 2 teaspoons baking powder. Stir in 1/3 cup grated cheese. Add 2 tablespoons lard and cut in as for biscuits. Add 1/3 cup milk. Pat out in a circle or square the size of a baking dish and cut in pie-shaped pieces. Place wedges of dough on top of meat mixture – slightly apart. Bake at 400° F for 30 minutes. Yields 5-6 servings.

PORK AND HAM LOAF

1½ lbs ground ham (not cooked)
½ lb ground lean pork
1 cup crumbled corn flakes (fine)
1 egg
1 tablespoon brown sugar
¼ teaspoon cloves
½ cup undiluted evaporated milk

Mix crumbs, eggs, sugar and cloves together. Add milk and ground meat and work together well. Pack in 2-lb loaf pan and bake at 325°F for 1½ hours. Cuts either hot or cold. Yields 6 servings.

HAM WITH SWEET POTATOES

1½ pounds sliced ham or shoulder
3 cups raw, sliced sweet potatoes
2 tablespoons sugar
1 cup hot water
1 tablespoon margarine

Cut the ham or shoulder into pieces for serving. If the meat is very salty, parboil it in water and drain. Brown the meat lightly on both sides and arrange the pieces to cover the bottom of a baking dish. Spread the sliced sweet potatoes over the meat, sprinkle with sugar. Add hot water to melted margarine and pour over the sweet potatoes and meat. Cover the dish and bake slowly until the meat and sweet potatoes are tender, basting the sweet potatoes occasionally with the gravy. Toward the last, remove the lid and let the top brown well. Yields 6 servings.

Modern adaptation: Heat oven to 350°F and place the ingredients in an 8 x 8-inch baking dish. Cover with aluminum foil and bake for approximately one hour, basting the sweet potatoes occasionally as directed in the original recipe. After baking for one hour remove foil and bake an additional 10 to 15 minutes or until the sweet potatoes have browned. Turkey ham may also be used, and the sugar can be decreased to one teaspoon.

HAM AND MACARONI AU GRATIN

2 cups cubed, cooked ham
2 cups cooked macaroni (1 cup raw)
1/4 cup butter or margarine
1/4 cup flour
2 cups milk
½ teaspoon salt
1/8 teaspoon pepper
1/2 cup grated cheese
1/2 cup cracker crumbs
2 tablespoons butter

Cook macaroni in boiling salted water for 20 minutes and drain. Mix with ham. Melt butter, add flour and stir in milk for sauce. Stir until sauce thickens. Season and add cheese. Arrange layers of the macaroni and ham mixture and the white sauce in a casserole and top with crumbs mixed with 2 tablespoons melted butter. Bake 30 minutes in 350°F oven. Makes 4-5 servings.

Modern adaptation: Bread crumbs may be used instead of cracker crumbs.

HAM MUFFINS

1/3 cup margarine, melted
1 medium-thick slice smoked ham
1 1/2 cups flour
3 tablespoons sugar
3 1/2 teaspoons baking powder
1 teaspoon salt
3/4 cup yellow cornmeal
1 cup milk
1 egg beaten

Dice ham and brown in skillet in its own fat. Sift flour, baking powder, sugar and salt together 3 times. Add cornmeal. Combine milk, egg and melted margarine. Add to dry ingredients and mix well. Place ham in bottom of each of 12 greased muffin tins. Cover with cornmeal mixture. Bake in hot oven (400°F) 25 minutes. Yield: 6 servings.

Modern adaptation: Since today's baking powders are all double-acting decrease baking powder to 1¾ teaspoons. If using a prepackaged diced ham browning in the skillet is not necessary unless seared ham pieces are desired. Turkey ham may also be used.

CELERY STUFFED SPARERIBS

1 side spareribs (about 1 1/2 lbs)
1/4 cup diced salt pork or bacon fat
1 cup chopped onion
1 cup chopped celery
3 cups soft bread cubes
3/4 teaspoon salt
1/8 teaspoon pepper

Fry the salt pork until crisp, then remove the pieces. Cook the onions in the fat for a few minutes, add the crisp salt pork, celery and bread cubes. Season with salt and pepper. Lay the spareribs over the dressing in baking pan, sprinkle the outside with 2 teaspoons salt and 1/8 teaspoon pepper and rub with flour. Place pan in 350°F oven uncovered and bake for 1½ to 2 hours or until ribs are tender. Yield: 4 servings.

Modern adaptation: Sliced bacon can be substituted for salt pork. (Bacon fat is another name for bacon grease.) Chop 4 to 6 slices of bacon and fry in a skillet or frying pan. Add onions and continue preparing the dressing as instructed in the original recipe. To help keep the dressing from getting too dry you may need to add ¼ to ½ cup of water or chicken stock. Once the spareribs are placed in the baking dish decrease salt to 1 teaspoon, or, for more zing, use 1 teaspoon of celery salt. Bake as directed in the original recipe.

PORK-U-PINES

1 lb pork sausage
1 lb lean fresh pork shoulder
1/2 teaspoon salt
1/2 cup raw rice
3 tablespoons flour
1 cup evaporated milk diluted with 1 cup water
1/8 teaspoon cloves
1/4 teaspoon cinnamon
1/4 teaspoon salt

Combine first four ingredients and shape into balls the size of golf balls. Brown slowly and thoroughly, turning often for 10-12 minutes. Add 1 cup water and simmer for 1¼ hours until all water is absorbed. Remove the balls, stir in flour, and add diluted evaporated milk. Season with cloves, cinnamon, and salt and add meatballs. Serve in the sauce. Yield: 6 servings.

Modern adaptation: For a richer gravy use the entire 12 ounce can of milk, diluting with 4 ounces of water or chicken stock. Ground turkey or turkey sausage can be used in place of pork. If using turkey cook the meatballs in 1 to 2 tablespoons of cooking oil. Can be served with rice, mashed potatoes or noodles.

BAKED SPARERIBS WITH SAUERKRAUT

1 1/2 lbs spareribs or 1 side
2 lbs (or about 1 quart) sauerkraut
1 1/2 teaspoon salt
1/8 teaspoon pepper

Place sauerkraut in large shallow baking dish. Rub spareribs with salt and pepper and arrange on top of sauerkraut. Bake in 350°F. oven for 1½ hours, or until brown and tender. Yield: 4 servings.

COUNTRY STYLE SALT PORK AND CREAM GRAVY

1 lb salt pork
(cut in 6-8 slices, depending on the length of the slab)
½ cup cornmeal

Soak pork in warm water for 20 minutes. Cover with cornmeal and fry over low heat for 20 minutes, draining off the fat as it accumulates. Make a cream gravy by blending 2 tablespoons fat with 2 tablespoons flour and stirring in 1 cup milk. When thickened, season to taste. Makes 4 servings.

Modern adaptation: Sliced ham can be used as a substitute for salt pork. Dip ham slices in egg, cover with corn meal, and fry in vegetable oil as directed in the original recipe, omitting the step of draining off the fat as it accumulates. Once the ham slices are brown on both sides remove from pan, and make the cream gravy as directed in the original recipe, using the pan drippings as the fat. Can be served over toast or biscuits.

PORK AND APPLE PIE

2 cups cooked pork (cut in cubes)
2 medium-sized tart apples (cored and sliced)
1 cup left-over gravy or thickened consommé

In a shallow baking dish, arrange alternate layers of pork and apples. Season each layer with a little salt and pepper. Pour over gravy. Top with strips of pastry made by blending ½ cup margarine with 1½ cups flour and ½ teaspoon salt. Add water to form stiff dough. Roll out to a sheet. Cut into strips. Bake in hot oven (400°F.)

Modern adaptation: Butter or shortening can be used instead of margarine. Bake for 25 to 30 minutes.

AMERICAN CHOP SUEY

1/2 to 1 lb lean pork or veal, cut up small
1 onion, sliced
2 cups cut-up celery
1 green pepper, chopped
3/4 cup uncooked rice
5 cups meat stock
(or 5 bouillon cubes and 5 cups boiling water)
1 to 2 teaspoons salt
1/8 teaspoon pepper
1 to 2 tablespoons chop suey sauce, (soy sauce) if desired

Brown pork or veal and onion in hot fat. Add celery, green pepper, rice, meat stock, salt and pepper and chop suey sauce. Cover, simmer 40 minutes. Uncover for last 15 minutes if you wish a thicker mixture.

SCALLOPED CORN AND SAUSAGE

1 lb pork sausages
3 tablespoons flour
1 1/2 cups milk
1/2 teaspoon salt
1/8 teaspoon pepper
1 pimiento, chopped
1 No. 2 can whole kernel corn*
1 cup cracker crumbs, fine

Fry pork sausage 6 to 7 minutes, or until lightly brown. Make 1½ cups white sauce by using 3 tablespoons sausage fat, blending in flour and adding milk gradually and stirring until thick. Season with salt and pepper and add chopped pimiento. Open whole kernel corn. Arrange cracker crumbs, corn, sausage and sauce in alternate layers, topping with crumbs mixed with 2 tablespoons sausage fat, and a row of 5 or 6 of the sausages. Bake 30 minutes in a 350°F oven. Makes 5 servings.

Modern adaptation: Prepare white sauce in a separate saucepan. If using a reduced fat sausage, use cooking oil or butter in place of sausage fat. Breadcrumbs may be used as a substitute for cracker crumbs. Bake in a 2-quart casserole dish.

** 2 ½ cups or 20 ounces*

BAKED SQUASH WITH SAUSAGE

Cut individual squash in half. Scrape cavity. Fill with bulk sausage. Place in baking pan and bake 1¼ hour in moderate oven (350°F).

SAUSAGE SHORTCAKES

½ lb bulk pork sausage
Bisquick

Season sausage, shape into patties and brown. Make biscuit dough from Bisquick. Roll thin—cut into rounds. Place each sausage patty between 2 rounds. Press edges together with fork. Prick tops. Bake 15 minutes on pan in hot oven (450°F). Serves 6.

OATMEAL COUNTRY SAUSAGE

1½ cups Quick Oats
1½ cups Old Fashioned Oats
3 cups boiling water
4 teaspoons salt
½ pound ground fat raw pork (ground pork)
½ Quick Oats, uncooked
4 teaspoons dry sage
1 teaspoon ground ginger
½ teaspoon thyme or other herb
margarine

Mix 1½ cup Old Fashioned Oats and boiling water seasoned with salt. Cook 3 minutes. Stir in pork and ½ cup uncooked Quick Oats. Season with sage, ginger and thyme. Allow to cool and then press into firm roll 3 inches in diameter. Sprinkle wax paper thickly with 1½ cup Quick Oats. Coat roll well with oats and roll up in the paper. Chill and slice about ½-inch thick. Remove wax paper. Sauté to golden brown in margarine. Serve hot.

CREAMED EGGS AND SAUSAGE

6 eggs
1/2 short stick sausage (1/4 lb)
1/3 cup butter
2 1/2 cups milk
1/3 cup flour
2 teaspoons Worcestershire sauce
salt and pepper
toast

Simmer eggs in water, cover for 20 minutes. Cool, peel and cut in quarters lengthwise. Cut sausage in tiny cubes ¼-inch square, cook, set aside. Melt butter, add flour, stir in milk and when thickened, add seasonings and Worcestershire sauce. Add eggs and sausage and let heat without stirring for 10-12 minutes. Serve over toast or English muffins. Makes 6 servings.

DUTCH POTATOES

6 medium potatoes
6 frankfurters
4 tablespoons drippings
salt and pepper
1 cup milk

Pare and remove centers of potatoes with apple corer. Draw a frankfurter through each. Place in an 8 x 12-inch baking pan. Mix milk, drippings, salt and pepper. Pour over potatoes. Bake 1 to 1¼ hours in a moderate oven (350°F). Serves 6.

MACARONI FRANKFURTER LOAF

6 frankfurters
2 cups uncooked elbow macaroni
2 cups grated American cheese
2 eggs, well beaten
1 cup milk
2 teaspoons salt

Cook macaroni in boiling salted water for 20 minutes. Drain. In loaf pan, combine macaroni with cheese, beaten eggs, milk and salt. Add frankfurters cut in ½-inch lengths. Bake in 350°F oven for 1 hour and 15 minutes or until solid. Keep top covered with wax paper most of cooking time to prevent drying. Turn out onto platter and garnish with tomato wedges or green vegetables. Yield: 6-7 servings.

Modern adaptation: Cook macaroni according to package directions. If using bun-length frankfurters decrease amount used to 3 or 4, depending on preference. Salt can be decreased to 1 teaspoon. A 9-inch loaf pan is suggested. Top with a thin layer of breadcrumbs. Cover with aluminum foil while baking.

PIGS IN BLANKETS

8 – 10 wieners or frankfurters
Bisquick

Simmer wieners in hot water for 10 minutes. Make Bisquick biscuit dough from package. Roll thin—cut in squares. Wrap wieners or franks (having ends show). Seal side edge by pinching together. Bake 15 minutes in hot oven. (450°F) Serves 8 – 10.

BOLOGNA CUPS WITH HOT POTATO SALAD

8 thin slices of Bologna (about ½ lb, leave casing on)
1/3 cup vinegar
1 egg
1/4 teaspoon mustard
1 teaspoon salt
1/8 teaspoon pepper
1 teaspoon sugar
1/4 cup bacon drippings
4 cups cubed potatoes, which have been cooked in boiling salted water
1/2 cup chopped green pepper
1/2 cup chopped onion

Place slices of Bologna in frying pan and heat gradually until the edges curl up to form a perfect cup. Fill with hot potato salad which has been made by adding vinegar, egg and seasonings to hot bacon drippings and pouring over hot potatoes, onion and green pepper. Makes 4 servings.

FULL O' BOLOGNEY

1½ cups sliced or cubed bologna
2 cups sliced or cubed raw potatoes
6 tablespoons flour
¼ teaspoon salt
¼ teaspoon pepper
3 tablespoons bacon fat (bacon grease)
2 cups milk

Arrange alternate layers of bologna, potatoes, flour, salt and pepper in a greased 7 or 8-inch baking dish. Dot with bacon fat,* pour milk on top. Bake 1 to 1¼ hours in moderate oven (350°F). Serves 4 – 6.

** Butter or margarine may be used as a substitute for bacon fat*

U.S. government poster. Circa 1942.

Poster for Mending Clothing. United States Government Printing Office.

Other WW2 Home Front History — Clothing Rationing

Most clothing, in the United States, was not rationed. However, those ladies who made their own clothes may have been limited on how many yards of fabric they could buy on a given day. There was, however, one fabric that was virtually unavailable during the war years. That fabric was nylon.

Nylon was needed to make parachutes, which meant ladies would have to do without nylon stockings. At that time stockings had seams on the back, so one solution to the hosiery shortage came from Max Factor, with a leg make-up that could draw a line down the back of the leg to simulate stocking seams. This solution however was not always practical. Drawing a straight line down the back of a leg took a certain amount of skill, and the make-up lines could smudge, especially in warm, humid weather.

Another option was rayon stockings. Rayon, however, proved to be a less than suitable substitute for nylon. Rayon stockings stretched and wrinkled very easily, and, when washed, they took an exceedingly long period of time to dry. A more practical, and popular, solution was bobby socks. Bobby socks remained a popular fashion accessory for teenaged girls until the 1960s.

"I remember riding the bus one day and noticing a woman getting up from her seat with smudges all over the back of her leg from wearing leg make-up."

— Bee Homes

20 UNITED STATES OF AMERICA 20
OFFICE OF PRICE ADMINISTRATION

RATION COUPON
FOR
TWENTY
POINTS
PROCESSED FOODS

20 OPA Form R-1325 ☆ GPO 20

CHAPTER FOUR

Poultry and Seafood

20 UNITED STATES OF AMERICA 20
OFFICE OF PRICE ADMINISTRATION

RATION COUPON
FOR
TWENTY
POINTS
MEAT, FATS, FISH, and CHEESES

20 OPA Form R-1015 ☆ GPO 20

Food rationing regulations were strict. A ration stamp could only be removed from the ration book in the presence of a storeowner or employee. Loose ration stamps were considered null and void and could not be used. If a family ran out of ration stamps they could not buy food until the next ration period began. And should a family member become ill and have to be hospitalized for a lengthy stay, his or her ration book would have to be turned in.

Food Raioning Poster. The United States Government Printing Office. Circa 1942.

SOUTHERN CHICKEN PIE

1½ cups chopped celery
½ cup chopped green pepper
½ cup sliced mushrooms (optional)
6 tablespoons butter
8 tablespoons enriched flour
4 cups milk (or half chicken broth and half milk)
3 cups cooked, sliced chicken

Pan-fry celery, green pepper, and mushrooms in butter until tender. Remove from butter; add flour; mix well. Add milk gradually, stirring constantly, until thickened. Add celery mixture and chicken; blend well. Season to taste. Turn into 2½ quart casserole or baking dish. Top with the following:

Baking Powder Biscuit Crust

2 cups sifted flour
3 teaspoons baking powder (or 2 teaspoons double-acting)*
½ teaspoon salt
¼ cup shortening
¾ milk

Sift flour once, measure; add baking powder and salt; sift together. Cut in shortening until mixture resembles coarse meal. Add milk all at once, mixing until all flour is dampened. Turn out on floured board; knead lightly for a few seconds to smooth out dough. Roll out to fit over casserole. Place over chicken mixture. Bake in hot oven (425° F) about 25 to 30 minutes until crust is done. Serve immediately. Serves 8 to 10.

Modern adaptation: Carrots can also be used. Dough can also be placed over chicken mixture dumpling style.

* *Most modern baking powder is double-acting.*

CHICKEN A LA KING

6 tablespoons margarine
6 tablespoons flour
1 cup milk or chicken broth
2 cups cream
1 green pepper, chopped
½ pound mushrooms, cut in pieces
1 teaspoon grated onion
3 egg yolks
salt
paprika
3 cups diced cooked chicken
½ cup finely chopped pimento

Make a white sauce with 5 tablespoons of margarine, the flour, the milk or broth, and 1½ cups of cream. In the other tablespoon of margarine, cook the green pepper, mushrooms, and onion over low heat for about 5 minutes. In the meantime beat the egg yolks, stir in the remaining ½ cup of cream, and add the mixture to the sauce. Do not overcook the sauce after the egg yolks are put in. Add the cooked vegetables, salt and paprika to taste, add the chicken and pimento. When the mixture is heated thoroughly, serve on crisp toast, in patty shells or toasted bread baskets, or on waffles, biscuits, or rice. Yields 6 servings.

CHICKEN CHOP SUEY

1 green pepper, shredded
2 cups shredded onion
2 tablespoons margarine
2 cups shredded celery
2 cups chicken broth
1 tablespoon cornstarch
1 tablespoon cold water
2 cups chopped cooked chicken
2 cups sliced Brazil nuts or Jerusalem artichokes
Soy sauce
Salt

Cook the green pepper and onion in the margarine for a few minutes. Add the celery, broth, mixed cornstarch and water, stir until smooth and slightly thickened, cover, and simmer for about 3 minutes. Add the chicken and nuts or artichokes, heat thoroughly. Season to taste with soy sauce and salt. Serve with hot flaky rice or fried noodles, on toast, with grits, or as a separate dish. Yields 6 servings.

CHICKEN-VEGETABLE CASSEROLE

6-8 tablespoons margarine
1 chicken, cut into pieces
2 tablespoons flour
2 cups water
12 mushrooms, sliced, if desired
6 onions, sliced
6 large potatoes, sliced thin
2 large carrots, sliced
Salt
Pepper

Sprinkle chicken pieces with salt and pepper and brown in part of the margarine over low heat. Place chicken in a well greased casserole. Add flour to drippings in pan and stir until brown. Add water gradually, stirring constantly and cook until thickened. Pour over chicken, cover and bake in hot oven (400°F) ½ hour. Meanwhile, brown sliced mushrooms and onions in remaining margarine over low heat. Remove chicken from casserole, arrange sliced potatoes and carrots in layers in casserole. Sprinkle each layer generously with salt. Top with browned mushrooms and onions. Lay chicken on top, sprinkle with paprika. Cover and bake ½ hour. Remove cover and bake 15 minutes to brown chicken. Yield: 6 servings.

CHICKEN TURNOVERS EN CASSEROLE

5 tablespoons fat drippings, melted
7 tablespoons enriched flour
1¼ teaspoon salt
½ teaspoon pepper
½ teaspoon celery salt
¼ teaspoon curry powder
1½ cups milk
1¼ cups chicken broth
¼ teaspoon Worcestershire sauce
2 cups cooked, diced potatoes
2½ cups (No. 2 can) string beans, well drained
1 cup cooked, diced carrots

Combine fat, flour, and seasonings in saucepan to make smooth paste. Add combined liquids gradually to flour mixture; stir constantly; cook until thick and smooth. Add Worcestershire sauce and vegetables. Turn into 12 x 8 x 2-inch casserole. Place in hot oven (425°F) for about 25 minutes to heat through. At the same time the following turnovers are baking:

Chicken Turnovers

3 tablespoons chopped onion
1 tablespoon fat or butter
¾ cup flaked, cooked chicken
½ teaspoon salt
1/8 teaspoon pepper
1½ cups sifted enriched flour
¾ teaspoon salt
½ cup shortening
4 to 5 tablespoons cold water

Pan-fry onions in fat until tender; remove from heat. Add chicken and seasonings. In mixing bowl, sift flour once, measure; add salt; sift again. Cut in shortening to about the size of small peas. Add water, a little at a time, until dough is moist enough to hold together; chill.

Roll out on a lightly floured board to about ¼-inch thickness. Cut with floured, chicken-shaped cutter into 12 pieces. Place about 2 tablespoons of above chicken mixture on half the pastry pieces. Moisten edges slightly; fit remaining pastry pieces over mixture. Seal edges with fork. Prick tops to allow escape of steam. Place on un-greased baking sheet. Bake in hot oven (425°F) for about 25 minutes. When done, arrange turnovers over top of casserole. Garnish with parsley and pimiento. Serve.

Note: If desired, turnovers may be made by cutting pastry into six 4-inch squares. Place chicken mixture on half of pastry; moisten edges slightly; fold over opposite edges; seal with fork.

CHICKEN AND RICE CUTLETS

2 tablespoons margarine
4 tablespoons flour
1 cup milk
2 eggs
1 cup boiled rice
1 cup chopped left-over chicken
bread crumbs

Melt margarine, blend with flour. Slowly stir in milk. Cook until thick. Stir in beaten egg. Remove from heat. Mix with rice and chicken. Season with salt and pepper. Spread in shallow pan; chill until stiff. Cut with biscuit cutter. Roll in crumbs, then dip in egg diluted with 2 tablespoons water, then in crumbs. Pan-fry in enough hot margarine to generously cover skillet until cutlets are brown.

Note: Allow the chicken mixture to chill for at least one hour before frying.

CHICKEN CROQUETTES

4 tablespoons margarine
5 tablespoons flour
1 cup milk
½ cup broth
3 cups ground or finely chopped cooked chicken
1 teaspoon finely chopped onion
1 tablespoon chopped parsley
salt and pepper
1 egg
1 tablespoon water
dry sifted bread crumbs
margarine for deep frying

Make a thick sauce with the margarine, flour, milk, and broth and let it stand until cold. When the sauce is cold, add the chicken, onion, parsley, and salt and pepper to taste. Mold the mixture into croquette shapes. Dip into the egg beaten with the water, roll in the bread crumbs, and allow to stand for an hour or longer in a cold place to dry the coating. Heat the margarine in a deep kettle to (350°F) or until an inch cube of bread browns in 40 seconds. Then carefully place several croquettes at a time in a frying basket, lower slowly into the margarine and cook until brown. Remove the fried croquettes and drain on absorbent paper. Serve hot with parsley garnish. Yields 6 servings.

NEW ENGLAND TURNOVERS

Turnover Filling

1 – 4 oz package shredded codfish
2 tablespoons margarine
2 tablespoons enriched all purpose flour
1/4 teaspoon pepper
1/2 cup milk

Freshen codfish as directed on package. Melt margarine over low heat. Add flour and seasoning and stir until smooth. Add milk, stirring consistently, until smooth and thickened. Add freshened codfish and mix well.

Pastry

1/2 cup margarine
1 cup sifted all-purpose flour
1/8 teaspoon salt
2 to 3 tablespoons water

Sift flour and salt together 3 times. Cut in margarine with a pastry blender or 2 knives until consistency of course meal. Add water and toss lightly with a fork until all particles are moistened. Roll out on lightly floured board into an 8 x 22-inch rectangle. Cut into 6 squares. Heap turnover filling into each square. Fold squares in half. Press edges together with fork dipped in flour. Prick top to allow steam to escape. Bake in hot oven (425°F) 15 minutes. Yield: 6 servings.

Modern adaptation: Fish can be freshened by placing it in a bowl of cold salt water for about 15 minutes. However, if using individually frozen pieces of uncooked fish, this step may not be necessary. Frozen pie shells or pastry can also be used, and any leftover filling can be served as a delicious topping over the turnovers.

FISH OR MEAT SOUFFLÉ

2 tablespoons butter, melted
4 tablespoons enriched flour
1 teaspoon salt
¼ teaspoon pepper
¼ teaspoon celery salt
¾ cup milk
4 egg yolks, well beaten
2 cups flaked salmon, tuna, ground, or cooked chopped meat
4 egg whites, stiffly beaten

Combine flour, butter, and seasonings in top part of double boiler. Add milk gradually, stirring constantly. Cook to form a thick paste.

Beat egg yolks until thick and light in color; add to flour mixture and stir until smooth. Add salmon; mix well. Fold carefully, but thoroughly, into egg whites beaten stiff but not dry. Turn into well-greased casserole. Place in pan of hot water; bake in moderate (350°F) oven about 1 hour and 10 minutes, or until set, or knife inserted into center comes clean. Serve at once with melted butter, celery, or pickle sauce. Serves 6.

Modern adaptation: For good results try using a 14.5 ounce can of salmon. To make a quiche combine the ingredients as directed in the original recipe and bake in a piecrust.

SAVORY SEAFOOD PIE

1 lb fresh fish (bass, trout, pickerel, etc.)
1/4cup chopped green pepper
1/4 cup chopped onion
1/2 cup chopped celery
2 tablespoons fat or drippings
1 3/4 teaspoon salt
1/8 teaspoon pepper
3/4 teaspoon Worcestershire sauce
1 tablespoon lemon juice
1 1/4 cups milk, scalded
2 eggs, slightly beaten
1 unbaked 9-inch pie shell

Boil fish in water about 15 minutes, or until tender. Remove bones and skin; break into 1-inch pieces. Pan-fry green pepper, onion, and celery in 2 tablespoons butter until tender. Add to fish. Add seasonings and lemon juice, mix. Combine milk and eggs. Add fish mixture. Turn into pastry-lined pan. Bake in hot oven (450°F) 15 minutes; reduce heat to moderate (350°F); bake until knife inserted in center comes out clean. Garnish with pimiento. Serve in wedge-shaped pieces. Serves 6.

BAKED STUFFED FILLETS

6 tablespoons margarine
6 fish fillets, (1½ pounds)
1½ cups hot mashed potatoes
2 tablespoons milk
1 teaspoon salt
¼ teaspoon pepper
3 tablespoons chopped onion

Mix potatoes with half the margarine, the milk, half the salt and onion. Mix remaining margarine, salt, and pepper and brush fish fillets generously. Arrange 3 fillets in a well greased baking dish. Spread potato stuffing on each fillet and cover with remaining fillets. Bake in a moderate oven (350°F) 25 minutes or until done. Yield: 6 servings.

Blue Star Banner Poster. United States Government Printing Office. Circa 1943.

Other WW2 Home Front History — Star in Service Banners

Long before yellow ribbons, families of servicemen and women kept special banners hanging in their windows. They were called Blue Star Service Banners, or Son in Service Banners, and they were a common sight in the windows of homes all across America. Each banner contained a red border with a blue star or stars in the center surrounded by a field of white. Each star represented a family member, usually a son or daughter, or sometimes a husband or a father, serving in the military. Some families had banners with one or two stars, while others may have had three, four or even more.

Then there was another banner. It looked like the others, but instead of a blue star it had a gold star. A gold star indicated a family member had made the ultimate sacrifice; a member had been killed in the line of duty. A mother who had lost a son was called a Gold Star Mother.

The most frightening sound in the world for any family with loved ones in the service must have been the sound of an unexpected knock at the door. If a loved one was lost in combat the military would send representatives to the home to notify the family in person. The United States lost some 292,000 soldiers in World War II. That would equal 292,000 Gold Stars.

"There was the devastating news of the five Sullivan brothers from Waterloo, Iowa, who all went down with their ship. It was hard to imagine how their parents could cope with such news."

— Marge Hackett

20 UNITED STATES OF AMERICA 20
OFFICE OF PRICE ADMINISTRATION

RATION COUPON
FOR
TWENTY
POINTS
PROCESSED FOODS

20 OPA Form R-1325 20

CHAPTER FIVE

Variety Meats

20 UNITED STATES OF AMERICA 20
OFFICE OF PRICE ADMINISTRATION

RATION COUPON
FOR
TWENTY
POINTS
MEAT, FATS, FISH, and CHEESES

20 OPA Form R-1015 20

Variety meats are nutritious. Make them delicious. Your family will like them if you fix them in interesting ways.

—*Your Share: How to prepare appetizing, healthful meals with foods available today,* Betty Crocker Home Service Staff, 1943

Times change and our eating choices change with them. While some of the ingredients in the recipes that follow may not be palatable for many of today's consumers, in past times meals made from these meats; liver, tongues, tails, hearts, and other organ meats, were more common. Even today, many of these meats are still popular in Europe and among various ethnic groups within the United States. There are, however, a few myths and misconceptions surrounding some of them. For instance, sweetbreads are not the pancreas of a cow. They are thymus glands of a calf or other young animal, and tripe comes from the stomach tissue.

These recipes have been included for their historical value and you may be surprised to discover a few old family recipes in the pages that follow. When appropriate, modern variations with suggestions for alternative ingredients have been included.

Those who wish to try these recipes in their original, historic format should be able to find many, if not most, of these meats available at supermarkets, butcher shops or food specialty stores.

LIVER AND VEGETABLE CASSEROLE

2 cups sifted flour
3/4 teaspoon baking powder (optional)
1 teaspoon salt
2/3 cup shortening
6 to 7 tablespoons cold water

Sift flour once, measure; add baking powder and salt; sift again. Cut in shortening until mixture resembles coarse meal. Add water, a little at a time, until dough is moist enough to hold together. Roll out about 2/3 of dough. Line bottom and sides of 12 x 8 x 2-inch baking dish. Fill with the following:

1/3 cup flour
1 1/2 teaspoons salt
1/4 teaspoon pepper
3 tablespoons fat, melted
1 cup vegetable broth
1 cup milk
1 3/4 cups (1 lb) cubed beef liver
1 teaspoon salt
3 tablespoons fat or butter
1 3/4 cups (about 2 medium) cooked, sliced potatoes
3/4 cups cooked, sliced carrots
1 cup cooked, sliced onions

Combine flour, salt, and pepper. Add 3 tablespoons fat; blend well. Add liquid (vegetable broth and milk) gradually; cook over direct heat until thick and smooth; stirring constantly.

Flour liver cubes; sprinkle with 1 teaspoon salt; pan-fry in 3 tablespoons of melted fat until nicely browned. Combine meat, vegetables, and sauce. Turn into pastry-lined baking dish. Roll out remaining pastry about 1/8-inch thick; cut out four 3 x 2-inch rectangles. Place one in each corner. Cut remaining pastry in ½-inch strips. Arrange attractively on open space of pie. Seal securely. Bake in hot oven (400°F) for about 40 minutes. Garnish with pimiento and parsley and serve immediately. Serves 6 to 8.

Modern adaptation: Round steak or chuck steak may be used instead of liver.

SPANISH LIVER

1 lb lamb, pork, or beef liver
1 1/2 tablespoon flour
1/2 onion
1/2 green pepper
1/2 clove garlic
1/2 cups mushrooms (if desired)
2 tablespoons butter or salad oil
No. 2 can tomatoes*
1 teaspoon salt
1/8 teaspoon pepper
3 cups cooked spaghetti

Dip liver in boiling water for 1-2 minutes, then cut into fine cubes and dredge with 1 ½ tablespoon flour. Chop onion, green pepper, garlic and mushrooms and let fry in butter or oil with the chopped liver until liver is lightly brown (about 10 minutes). Add tomatoes and seasonings and cover. Cook slowly for 20-25 minutes. Serve over boiled spaghetti with a sprinkling of grated Italian style cheese over the top. Makes 4 servings.

** 2 ½ cups or 20 ounces.*

CRISPY LIVER STEAKS

1 lb lamb's liver, sliced
1 cup cracker crumbs
1 egg
1 tablespoon lemon juice
½ teaspoon salt
2 tablespoons butter

***Catsup Sauce**

2 tablespoons butter
2 tablespoons catsup

Dip slices of liver first in cracker crumbs, then in egg beaten with the lemon, 1 tablespoon water and salt. Dip again in cracker crumbs. Brown on both sides in butter. Serve with catsup sauce made by beating sauce ingredients and ½ cup water together. Makes 4 servings.

Modern adaptation: Chicken livers or beef liver can be used in place of lamb's liver. Try serving with barbeque sauce.

* *Catsup is a variation of the word ketchup.*

LIVER LOAF

1 1/2 lbs pork liver or lamb's liver
4 slices bacon
1/2 cup chopped onion
2 1/2 cups soft bread crumbs
2 eggs
1/4 cup chopped parsley
2 teaspoons salt
1/8 teaspoon pepper

Let slices of liver stand in hot water for 10 minutes and then grind* with the onion and bacon. Add eggs, crumbs, parsley and seasonings. Mix well and pack firmly into loaf pan. Bake 1 hour at 350°F. Serve with creamed potatoes. May be sliced cold. Yield: 6-7 servings.

**If you don't have a meat grinder, a food processor will substitute.*

LIVER SAUSAGE LOAF

3 strips bacon
3 tablespoons chopped onion
1 lb liver sausage
2 eggs
2 cups soft, fresh bread crumbs
2 tablespoons chopped parsley
¾ teaspoon salt

Lightly fry bacon and onion. Cut bacon fine and add fat, onion and bacon to 1 lb liver sausage that has been minced with a fork. Add eggs, bread crumbs, parsley and salt. Mix well and press into a loaf pan. Bake 35 minutes in a 350°F oven. Serve with whole creamed potatoes surrounding the loaf. Makes 5-6 servings.

LIVER PATTIES

1 lb pork liver
½ cup chopped onion
1 egg
1½ teaspoon salt
¾ cup dry bread crumbs
2 tablespoons butter, lard or drippings

Allow liver to stand in hot water 10 minutes and coarsely grind. Mix with onion, egg, salt and bread crumbs. Form into 8 small patties about ¾-inch thick, brown in fat. Cook for about 6 minutes per side. Too long cooking will develop a strong flavor. Patties may be wrapped in bacon and broiled. Makes 8 patties.

LIVERWURST PIE

4 tablespoons margarine
2 cups sifted flour
4 teaspoons baking powder
1/2 teaspoon salt
2/3 to 3/4 cup liquid (half milk and half water)
1 pound liverwurst

Measure flour. Add baking powder and salt and sift together three times. Cut in margarine, using a pastry blender or 2 knives, until of consistency of course meal. Add liquid and stir until soft dough forms. Place on lightly floured board and knead lightly until smooth on one side. Cut off a small portion of the dough and fit into an 8-inch pie plate. Mash liverwurst and press firmly into pie plate. Roll remaining piece of dough and cut with a tiny biscuit cutter or sharp knife. Place on top of liverwurst. Bake in a hot oven, (400°F) 30 minutes. Yield: 6 servings.

OXTAILS WITH HORSERADISH

1 oxtail (about 1 1/2 lbs)
1 tablespoon lard
1 teaspoon salt

Horseradish Sauce

1 tablespoon butter
1 tablespoon flour
1 1/4 teaspoon salt
1/2 cup bottled horseradish
1/8 teaspoon pepper
1/2 cup evaporated milk diluted with ½ cup water

Have oxtail cut in short lengths. Melt fat in heavy frying pan and brown oxtail. Add 1 cup water, and salt and simmer about 2 ½ hours. In another pan melt the butter. Blend in flour, salt, pepper and horseradish. Add milk gradually and stir until thick. To serve, pour horseradish sauce over the braised oxtails. Makes 4 servings.

BRAISED OXTAILS

2 lbs oxtails, separated at joints
4 tablespoons fat
1 teaspoon salt
¼ teaspoon pepper
2 cups water
1 cup cut-up carrots
1 cup cut-up potatoes
½ cup cut-up celery
½ cup cut-up onion

Brown oxtails in fat. Add salt and pepper and water. Simmer covered 3½ hours. Add more water if necessary. Add carrots, potatoes, celery and onion. Continue cooking until tender (30 minutes to 1 hour). Thicken juice with small amounts of flour before serving. Serves 4.

BRAISED OX JOINTS

1 oxtail
2 tablespoons butter
1 cup canned tomatoes
1 teaspoon salt
1/8 teaspoon pepper
1 teaspoon celery salt
4 whole cloves
1 bay leaf
3 cups diced carrots (about 4 carrots)
2 small onions, chopped
1/2 clove of garlic
1/4 cup diced turnips
1/4 cup lemon juice

Cut oxtail in short lengths, roll in flour and brown slowly in 1 tablespoon butter about 15 minutes. Add 1 cup water, tomatoes and seasonings, simmer about 2 hours or until tender. Brown carrots, onions, garlic and turnips in 1 tablespoon butter 3-4 minutes; add to meat and cook ½ hour longer. Add lemon juice the last 10 minutes of cooking. Yield: 4 servings.

PORK TAILS AND LIMA BEANS

2 lbs pork tails (4 tails) cut in short lengths
1 cup dried lima beans (soaked several hours)
2 teaspoons salt
1 small onion
2 tablespoons vinegar

Simmer tails, beans, salt and onion slowly for 2 to $2^{1}/_{2}$ hours, add $2^{1}/3$ cups water to which has been added 2 tablespoons vinegar. Add more water if desired. Serve with a crisp green salad. Makes 4 servings.

Modern adaptation: If pork tails are not available cheaper cuts of pork, such as pork shoulder, can be used. For more flavor use chicken stock instead of water, and white wine vinegar. Omit salt if using chicken stock.

SCRAMBLED BRAINS AND EGGS

1 calf's brain (about 1 lb)*
1/4 cup butter
5 eggs, beaten slightly
1 teaspoon salt
1/8 teaspoon pepper
1 tablespoon Worcestershire sauce
2 tablespoons tomato catsup
2 tablespoons chopped parsley
{lemon juice or vinegar}

Wash brains thoroughly and remove as much of the membrane as possible. Soak ½ hour in salted water. Drain and simmer 20 minutes in water to which 1 teaspoon of salt and 1 teaspoon of lemon juice or vinegar has been added for each quart of water. Drain and cook in cold water. Melt butter in heavy skillet, combine brains with other ingredients and stir with fork until eggs are lightly set. Yield: 6 servings.

** Pork brains may also be used.*

VEAL HEART WITH NOODLES

2 veal hearts (about 2 lbs)
3 tablespoons flour
2 tablespoons butter or margarine
2 cups sliced onion
2 teaspoons salt
1/8 teaspoon pepper
4 cups cooked noodles

Split heart open, remove arteries and veins and wash thoroughly. Cut in small pieces, dust with flour and brown in butter or margarine. Add onions, ½ cup water* and seasonings and simmer until tender or about 2 hours. Arrange hearts on noodles and pour liquid over top. Makes 6-7 servings.

Modern Adaptation: Skirt steak or chuck steak can be used instead of hearts. If using a steak cooking time can be decreased to 45 minutes to one hour. Red wine can also be used in place of water, and olive oil may be used instead of butter.

**Small amounts of water may need to be added periodically during cooking time.*

HEART CHOP SUEY

1 small beef heart (3 lbs) or 2 small veal hearts (2 lbs)
3 tablespoons flour
2 cups coarsely chopped onion
¼ cup butter or margarine
1 cup diced celery
½ coarsely chopped green pepper
2 bouillon cubes
2 teaspoons salt
¼ teaspoon pepper
2 tablespoons Worcestershire sauce
4 cups boiled rice

Split heart open, remove arteries and veins, and wash thoroughly. Cut into ½-inch cubes and dust with flour. Place meat and onion in heavy frying pan and brown in butter or margarine. Add celery, green pepper and bouillon cubes and 2 cups water. Cover and simmer until tender, about 1 to 1½ hours. Add seasonings and sauce. Serve with boiled rice or fried Chinese Noodles. Yields 6-8 servings.

Modern adaptation: Stew meat or chuck steak can be used as a substitute for beef or veal hearts. Beef or chicken stock can be used in place of water and bouillon cubes. If using stock omit salt.

STUFFED BEEF HEART

1 beef heart (3 ½ lbs)
1 tablespoon salt
¼ cup vinegar

Dressing

½ cup celery
2½ cups fine, dry bread crumbs
2 tablespoons onion
¼ cup green pepper
1 teaspoon salt
2 tablespoons butter

Remove all valves and blood vessels from heart. Soak in cold, salted water ½ hour. Drain. Simmer slowly in water to cover 3-4 hours or until tender. Add vinegar last half hour of cooking time. Combine ingredients for dressing and ½ cup water. Stuff heart. Bake for 40 minutes in 325°F oven. Makes 6-8 servings.

BEEF AND KIDNEY PIES

1 lb beef chuck or round steak
1 beef kidney*
2 tablespoons lard or butter
1 cup diced onions
1 1/2 teaspoon salt
1/8 teaspoon pepper
2 teaspoons Worcestershire sauce
2 tablespoons flour

Soak kidney in cold salted water for 30 minutes. Cut beef in 1-inch cubes. Drain kidney and cut into small cubes. Brown diced onions slowly in lard or butter; add meats and brown well on all sides. Add salt, pepper, Worcestershire sauce and 2 cups boiling water. Simmer slowly for 2½ hours or until very tender. Mix flour with ¼ cup cold water and stir into meat mixture to thicken. Transfer to individual casseroles and cover each with thin pastry. Make holes in centers for escape of steam. Bake 30 minutes in 325ºF oven. Makes 4 individuals pies.

Modern Adaptation: Premade or ready-made pie shells may be used as a pastry.

** To prepare kidneys first wash and remove any membrane. Split through center, lengthwise and remove fat and heavy veins. Soak in cold salted water as directed above.*

KIDNEY STEW

2 beef kidneys (approximately 2 lbs)*
¼ cup flour
2 teaspoons salt
2 tablespoons butter, lard or margarine
4 tablespoons minced onion
½ cup red cooking wine

Split kidneys and remove all the fatty tissue. Cut into 1-inch pieces and soak in salt water for 1 hour. Mix the flour and salt and dust the kidneys with the mixture. Brown slowly in fat. Add the onions. When brown add 2 cups water. Simmer for 1½ hours. Add the wine and cook only long enough to heat the wine. If necessary, thicken the gravy with 1 tablespoon flour mixed with ¼ cup cold water. Serve on rice or in pastry shells. Makes 4-6 servings.

* *To prepare kidneys first wash and remove any membrane. Split through center, lengthwise and remove fat and heavy veins. Soak in cold salted water as directed above.*

PORK KIDNEYS WITH EGGS

2 pork kidneys
2 tablespoons flour
2 tablespoons butter or margarine
paprika
1/2 teaspoon salt
1/8 teaspoon pepper
4 eggs
4 tablespoons milk

Cut kidneys in half. Remove outer membrane and heavy veins. Soak for 1 hour in cold, salted water. Dry. Cut into thin slices. Dust slices lightly with flour and cook slowly in butter or margarine for 30 minutes. Season with salt, pepper and paprika. Beat the eggs and add the milk. Cook in butter or margarine until done. Place scrambled eggs in center of platter with kidneys in border around them. Yield: 3-4 servings.

BROILED SWEETBREADS WITH TARTER SAUCE

1 lb sweetbreads
½ cup tarter sauce or mayonnaise
dry bread crumbs

Soak sweetbreads ½ hour in cold, salted water. Place in 1 quart of water to which 1 teaspoon lemon juice and 1 teaspoon salt have been added and let simmer for 30 minutes. Remove all membranes and split in half lengthwise or break in two. Dip in tarter sauce or mayonnaise and then in dry bread crumbs. Place on broiler pan 4-5 inches under heat. Broil 6 to 8 minutes to the side. Yield: 4 servings.

BREADED SWEETBREADS

1 lb sweetbreads
1 sprig parsley
1/3 cups chopped celery
1 teaspoon salt
1 teaspoon lemon juice
1 egg, slightly beaten
1 cup bread crumbs
2 tablespoons butter

Soak sweetbreads ½ hour in salted water. Drain, remove any loose membranes, and place in saucepan with parsley, celery, salt, lemon juice and enough water to cover. Simmer 30 minutes. Remove fat and connective tissue from sweetbreads. Split lengthwise. Dip in bread crumbs, then in egg and again in crumbs. Fry quickly in melted butter. Serve with tomato sauce. Makes 4 servings.

HAM AND SWEETBREADS IN PASTRY SHELLS

¾ cup precooked sweetbreads (1/4 lb)
¾ cup cubed, cooked ham (1/4 lb)
2 tablespoons butter or ham fat
2 tablespoons flour
½ teaspoon salt
½ cup evaporated milk diluted with ½ cup water
¼ cup chopped green pepper
¼ cup roasted almonds, or other salted nuts

Pre-cook sweetbreads by soaking for 30 minutes in cold water, then simmering for 20 minutes in water to which 3 tablespoons vinegar and 1 teaspoon salt have been added. Remove membranes and cube.

Melt fat, add flour and salt and stir in milk, stirring until the sauce thickens. Add green pepper and meats and heat 10-15 minutes. Serve in pastry shells topped with sliced, salted nuts. Yields 4-5 servings.

To make pastry shells: Use regular pie crust, roll in 6-inch circles and bake over the back of medium-sized muffin tins.

BOILED FRESH TONGUE AND SPINACH

1 beef tongue (about 4 lbs)
4 teaspoons salt
3 lbs spinach

Cover tongue with water and let simmer in covered container 3-4 hours, or until tender. When half done add salt. 15 minutes before done, add spinach and leave container uncovered. Remove skin and roots from hot tongue, slice and serve on platter with spinach. Makes 4 servings per pound of meat.

TONGUE GOULASH

4 thick slices of cooked beef tongue or 2 whole lamb tongues cut in 1-inch pieces*
2 tablespoons flour
2 tablespoons butter
1/2 cup chopped onions
2 cups tomatoes, or a No. 1 can tomatoes
4 medium-sized potatoes cut in large pieces
1 tablespoon chopped parsley
1/8 teaspoon curry powder
1 1/2 teaspoons salt
1/8 teaspoon pepper

Dust tongue with flour and brown with onions in melted butter in Dutch oven. Add remaining ingredients and simmer until tender or about 45 minutes. Makes 4 servings.

Modern adaptation: Chuck steak may be used as a substitute for tongue. For added flavor try adding ½ cup red wine. A 14.5 ounce can of chopped or diced tomatoes will work with this recipe. A skillet, or electric skillet, may be used instead of a Dutch oven.

** To prepare tongue wash and cover with hot, salted water. Cook until tender, about 2 hours for pork, veal or lamb tongues, 3 hours for beef tongues. Allow tongue to cool in liquid. Remove connective tissue, roots and skin.*

PHILADELPHIA PEPPER POT

4 slices bacon
1 lb honeycomb tripe
1 onion, chopped
1 green pepper, chopped
2 quarts soup stock, or 2 quarts water and 6 bouillon cubes
1 teaspoon salt
½ teaspoon pepper
1 cup diced potatoes
2 tablespoons flour
2 tablespoons butter

Cut the bacon into small cubes and fry until golden brown. Add onion and green pepper, and cook slowly for 5 minutes. Add soup stock and tripe which has been washed and shredded. Season with salt and pepper and bring to a boiling point. Add potatoes and simmer 1 hour. Thicken with flour and butter which have been creamed together. Just before serving add ½ cup evaporated milk. Makes 4 servings.

FRENCH FRIED TRIPE

1 lb fresh tripe
1 cup flour
1 ½ teaspoon baking powder
½ teaspoon salt
1 egg
1 cup milk
1 tablespoon melted fat

Wash tripe thoroughly and simmer in salted water until tender (about 1 hour). Drain and cut in 1-inch pieces. Sift dry ingredients together. Combine the beaten egg, milk and fat. Add gradually to the dry ingredients, stirring only until smooth. Dip tripe in batter and deep fat fry at 375°F until brown. Makes 4 servings.

TRIPE NEW ORLEANS

1 lb fresh honeycomb tripe
2 tablespoons drippings or mayonnaise
½ cup chopped onions
¼ cup chopped green pepper
1 cup tomato puree or one 8 oz short can
1 teaspoon salt
½ teaspoon paprika
1 tablespoon Worcestershire sauce
1 tablespoon flour

Wash tripe thoroughly and simmer in salted water until tender (about 1 hour.) Drain. Brown onion in drippings, add tomato puree, green pepper, seasonings and tripe that has been cut in 1-inch pieces. Make paste of flour and 2 tablespoons water, and add to tripe mixture. Stir until thick. Make a rice ring on platter. Pour tripe in center of rice ring. Makes 4-5 servings.

Food Rationing Poster. United States Government Printing Office. Circa 1943.

Civil Defense Poster. United States Government Printing Office. Circa 1942.

Other WW2 Home Front History — Civil Defense

The attack on Pearl Harbor shocked and stunned the nation. In the weeks and months that followed there was a genuine fear that the Japanese or the Germans might attack the United States mainland as well. People living in coastal areas were particularly concerned. The Office of Civilian Defense responded to this emergency by recruiting thousands of volunteers nationwide and mobilizing the nation to prepare for a possible enemy attack by air or sea. There were even preparations made for gas attacks. Every neighborhood had a volunteer Air Raid Warden whose job was to be sure that everyone in his neighborhood was prepared. The Air Raid Wardens enforced black outs and organized air raid drills while Civil Defense volunteers watched the skies and seas.

"My dad was the neighborhood Air Raid Warden. I remember he always wore a suit and tie with his Civil Defense armband and helmet. He would patrol our neighborhood and if he saw anyone with their lights on at night he would knock on their door and ask them to turn their lights out. Everyone was friendly and cooperative. They would usually invite him in for a cup of coffee."

— Jim Easterbrook

20 UNITED STATES OF AMERICA 20
OFFICE OF PRICE ADMINISTRATION

RATION COUPON
FOR
TWENTY
POINTS
MEAT, FATS, FISH, and CHEESES

20 OPA Form R-1615 20

CHAPTER SIX

VEGETABLES, CHEESE AND MEATLESS MAIN DISHES

20 UNITED STATES OF AMERICA 20
OFFICE OF PRICE ADMINISTRATION

RATION COUPON
FOR
TWENTY
POINTS
PROCESSED FOODS

20 OPA Form R-1325 20

Another means of conserving meat during the war years was Meatless Tuesday. Each Tuesday grocers removed what meat they had from their meat cases, and restaurants would not serve meat. Imagine the embarrassment of walking into a diner or cafe, forgetting it was Tuesday, and ordering a ham sandwich. Homemakers also needed to find meat substitutes, so cheese or vegetable dishes would be the main course on Tuesdays.

Vegetables were less affected by rationing. Many families grew their own fruits and vegetables in their backyard Victory Gardens, which they would home can for later use. Fresh fruits and vegetables, when available, were not rationed.

Victory Garden Poster. United States Government Printing Office. Circa 1943.

CHEESE SOUFFLÉ

1½ cups milk
1 cup bread crumbs
1 tablespoon margarine
4 eggs
1½ pound cheese, shaved thin (2 cups)
¼ teaspoon salt
pepper to taste

Heat the milk, bread crumbs, and margarine in a double boiler. For the crumbs, crumble up the left-over pieces of bread and pack the measure well. Do not use fine, very dry crumbs. Add cheese to the hot mixture. Stir until the cheese has melted. Add this mixture to the well-beaten egg yolks. Season. Fold hot mixture into the stiffly beaten egg whites containing the salt. Pour into a greased dish and bake very slow for 1 hour, or until set in the center. Yields 6 servings.

CHEESE FONDUE

1 cup bread crumbs
1 cup grated sharp cheese
1 beaten egg
1 cup milk
1/2 teaspoon salt
1/16 teaspoon of pepper
1/8 teaspoon dry mustard

Place bread crumbs and cheese in layers in an 8-inched greased casserole. Mix and pour in beaten egg, milk, salt and pepper and dry mustard. Bake for 40 minutes in moderate oven (350°F). Serves 6.

TOMATO RAREBIT

2 tablespoons margarine
½ small onion, chopped
½ green pepper, chopped, if desired
½ cup finely cut celery, if desired
2 tablespoons flour
1 pint tomatoes
½ pound cheese, shaved thin (2 cups)
1 teaspoon salt
2 eggs, well beaten

Melt margarine in a heavy skillet. Stir in onion, celery, and pepper. Cook a few minutes, stirring frequently. Add the flour, tomatoes, cheese, and salt. Stir and cook over low heat until the mixture thickens and the cheese melts. Pour some of this mixture into well-beaten eggs. Pour all back into skillet and cook until thickened and creamy. Serve on toast or crackers. Yields 6 servings.

FAVORITE CHEESE CASSEROLE

12 slices enriched bread
½ lb sharp cheese, cut in ½-inch slices
4 egg yolks, beaten
1½ cups milk
1 teaspoon salt
½ teaspoon pepper
¼ teaspoon dry mustard

Arrange 6 slices of bread in 8x12-inch baking dish. Cover with sliced cheese. Top with remaining 6 slices of bread. Mix egg yolks, milk, salt and pepper and dry mustard, pour over top. Chill. Bake 1 hour in moderate oven (350°F). Yield: 6-8 servings.

CHEESE AND MACARONI LOAF WITH RAREBIT SAUCE

1 cup elbow macaroni
3 tablespoons margarine
3 tablespoons flour
1 teaspoon salt
¼ teaspoon dry mustard
Dash of pepper
1¼ cups milk
1 cup (4-oz) shredded American cheese
1 teaspoon Worcestershire sauce
2 eggs, well beaten
1¼ cups chopped green pepper

Cook macaroni in large amounts of rapidly boiling salted water until tender, drain.

Melt margarine. Blend in flour and seasonings. Remove from heat. Add milk gradually, mixing well. Cook over low heat, stirring until thickened. Add cheese, stirring until melted. Add Worcestershire sauce to well-beaten eggs, add macaroni, green pepper, and half of cheese sauce, mix well. (Place rest of sauce over hot water.) Pour macaroni mixture into well-greased loaf pan (8 x 4 x 2 ½ inches). Bake in a moderate oven (350ºF) about 45 minutes. Turn out on warm platter. Garnish with water cress and broiled tomato slices, seasoned with grated onion, salt and pepper. Serve loaf, sliced, with remaining cheese sauce. Serves 6.

OPEN CHEESE SANDWICHES

2 eggs, well beaten
2 cups grated sharp cheese
1 teaspoon Worcestershire sauce
½ teaspoon salt
¼ teaspoon paprika
6 slices of bread
2 half strips bacon

Combine eggs, cheese, Worcestershire sauce, salt and paprika. Spread on 6 slices of bread, toasted on bottom side. Top with bacon. Broil 8 – 10 minutes, until cheese melts and bacon is crisp. Makes 6 servings.

GNOCCHI

¾ cup milk or water
2 tablespoons butter
1 cup sifted flour
½ cup grated sharp cheese
½ teaspoon salt
¼ teaspoon paprika
2 eggs

Heat water and butter to boil. Reduce heat. Add flour all at once and stir vigorously until mixture leaves sides of pan and forms into a soft ball of dough. Remove from heat. Blend in cheese, salt and paprika, then add two unbeaten eggs, one at a time. Mix thoroughly. Divide into 12 parts. Dip into flour, pat into cake (1/4-inch thick). Chill. Brown in hot pan. Sprinkle with cheese. Serve with tomato sauce.

VEGETABLE SOUFFLÉ

3 tablespoons margarine
3 tablespoons enriched all-purpose flour
1 teaspoon salt
1/4 teaspoon pepper
1/3 cup milk
3 eggs, separated
1 cup cooked, chopped spinach
1 cup cooked, chopped carrots

Melt margarine over low heat. Add flour and seasonings and mix well. Add milk gradually, stirring constantly until smooth and thickened. Add well-beaten egg yolks and vegetables. Fold in stiffly beaten egg whites. Bake in individual greased casseroles set in a pan of hot water in a moderate oven (350°F) 30 minutes. Yield: 6 servings.

POTAGE DE FROMAGE

3 lb soup bone
$2^1/_4$ quarts water
2 bay leaves
1 sliced onion
2 teaspoons salt
$^1/_8$ teaspoon pepper
$^1/_2$ teaspoon celery seed
$^1/_8$ teaspoon thyme
12 slices dry toast
$^1/_2$ to 1 lb sharp cheese
2 eggs, slightly beaten
$^1/_4$ cup cooking brandy

Cover soup bone with water. Add bay leaves, onion, salt and pepper, celery seed and thyme. Simmer 3 hours and remove bone. Place dry toast and cheese in alternate layers in deep kettle. Pour in 2 quarts of hot, unstrained broth. Blend in eggs and cooking brandy. Heat in slow moderate oven (325°F) until heated through. Serves 8.

BAKED KIDNEY BEANS

2 cups dry red kidney beans
1 large onion, sliced
1 large clove garlic
1 green pepper, minced
½ cup bacon drippings
2 cups tomato juice or 1 No. 2 can tomatoes*
2 teaspoons salt
1½ teaspoon chili powder

Soak beans overnight or cover with water and bring to boiling point, remove from the stove and allow to soak for 45 minutes. Drain, cover with 1½ quarts water. Add all other ingredients except chili powder and simmer for 2 hours. Add more water if necessary. Add the chili powder, stirring as little as possible to avoid mashing the beans. Place in a covered casserole or bean pot and bake for 2 more hours. Uncover the last of the cooking time if brown beans are desired. Yield: 5-6 servings.

** 2 ½ cups or 20 ounces.*

PLENTIFUL POT PIE

3 tablespoons fat*
5 tablespoons flour
1 teaspoon salt
1 teaspoon celery salt
½ teaspoon paprika
3 bouillon cubes
3 cups boiling water
16 small onions, cooked
1 cup left-over vegetables
1 cup lima beans, cooked
1 cup sliced carrots, cooked

Melt fat. Blend in flour, salt, celery salt and paprika. Add bouillon cubes dissolved in boiling water. Add onions, left-over vegetables, lima beans and carrots. Place in 8 x 12-inch baking dish. Cover with Bisquick topping, (see Meat Pie Topping on Bisquick package.) Bake 15 to 20 minutes in hot oven. (425°F to 450°F) Serves 6.

Modern Adaptation: Beef broth or stock may be used in place of boullion cubes and boiling water. Prepackaged bicuits or pie crust can be used instead of Bisquick topping.

* *Butter, margarine, Crisco or lard may be used as a fat.*

SAVORY VEGETABLE PIE

2 tablespoons melted fat*
$^{2}/_{3}$ cup thinly sliced onions
$^{2}/_{3}$ cup sliced celery
1 $^{2}/_{3}$ cups cooked vegetables (peas, string beans, and carrots)
$3^{1}/_{2}$ tablespoons flour
$^{1}/_{2}$ teaspoon salt
dash of pepper
$2^{1}/_{4}$ cups milk and vegetable stock
1 teaspoon vinegar
1 teaspoon Worcestershire sauce
3 hard-cooked eggs, sliced
1 recipe Savory Biscuits (see Chapter 7, page 155)

Melt fat in skillet, add onions and celery, and cook gently 10 minutes. Add cooked vegetables.

Combine flour, salt, and pepper; add to melted fat in saucepan and blend. Add liquid gradually and cook gently until thickened, stirring constantly. Add the onions and celery, vinegar, and Worcestershire sauce. Turn half of mixture into shallow baking dish. Cover with egg slices, sprinkle with salt and pepper, and top with remaining vegetable mixture.

Mix biscuit dough as directed. (See Chapter 7) Drop or place biscuits on vegetable mixture. Bake in hot oven (425°F) 25 minutes. Serves 4.

Modern adaptation: Prepacked biscuits may be used. Bisquick biscuits would also be suitable.

* *Butter, margarine, cooking oil or lard may be used as a fat.*

VEGETABLE TRAY

Cauliflower
Margarine
Cooked carrot strips
Salt, pepper
Tomatoes
Whole kernel corn, canned or fresh cooked

Cook the cauliflower whole, without removing all of the small, tender leaves. Drain well and place in the center of a serving tray or chop plate. Season with a generous amount of softened margarine. Surround with cooked carrot strips tossed in melted margarine, and baked tomatoes with part of the centers scooped out and filled with corn seasoned with salt and pepper and melted margarine.

VARIETY CHOP PLATE

4 tablespoons margarine
6 mashed potatoes
1/4 cup milk
1/2 teaspoon salt
1/8 teaspoon pepper
1 tablespoon chopped parsley
6 eggs

Beat potatoes, margarine, milk, seasonings and parsley until fluffy. Form 6 potato nests in greased pan. Break egg into each nest. Bake at 350°F 12 minutes. Serve with cabbage and carrots. Yield: 6 servings.

VICTORY VEGETABLE PLATE

2 1/2 cups sifted enriched flour
3 3/4 teaspoons baking powder (or 2 1/2 teaspoons double acting)*
3/4 teaspoon salt
1/3 cup shortening
1 cup milk
1 1/2 cups (1/4 lb) grated nippy cheese*
3 cups fresh or canned cooked mixed vegetables (potatoes, carrots, peas, beans, beets, corn or lima beans)

Sift flour once, measure; add baking powder and salt; sift again. Cut in shortening until mixture resembles coarse meal. Add milk all at once; mix until all flour is dampened. Knead on floured board a few seconds to smooth surface. Pat or roll out into rectangle 10 x 8 inches. Spread with cheese. Roll up as for jelly roll, the long way of the dough. Cut into six slices. Place on greased baking sheet, cut side up. Flatten out and shape each piece into 3½ inches in diameter. Bake in hot (450°F) oven about 25 minutes. Serve with hot buttered and seasoned vegetables and the following tomato sauce.

Tomato Sauce

3 tablespoons fat or drippings
4 tablespoons enriched flour
2 teaspoons salt
2 teaspoons sugar
¼ teaspoon pepper
¼ teaspoon chili powder (optional)
3½ cups (No. 2 can) tomatoes, juice and pulp

Combine fat, flour and seasonings in saucepan. Add tomatoes gradually, stirring constantly. Cook over direct heat until thick and smooth. Serves 6.

*Nippy Cheese

1 (3 oz) package cream cheese
1 tablespoon mayonnaise
1 tablespoon heavy cream
2 tablespoons sweet pickle relish
1 tablespoon finely chopped onion or onion powder
1 teaspoon prepared horseradish sauce
3 drops hot pepper sauce
1/8 teaspoon garlic salt

Beat together cream cheese, mayonnaise and heavy cream in a mixing bowl until smooth. Mix in sweet pickle relish, onion, horseradish, hot pepper and garlic salt. Cover and chill in the refrigerator for at least one hour, move to serving bowl before serving.

VEGETABLE POTPOURRI

1½ cups cut cabbage
1 cup sliced carrots
½ cup chopped onions
½ cup chopped celery
¼ teaspoon salt
½ cup boiling water

Combine and cook until tender. (20 minutes.) Makes 4 servings.

Modern adaptation: Omit salt and use ½ cup of chicken stock instead of ½ cup of water.

VEGETABLE STEW WITH NUTMEG DUMPLINGS

4 tablespoons margarine
1 green pepper
¾ cup scallions or onions
3 bouillon cubes
4 cups boiling water
¼ cup dried or fresh celery leaves
2 teaspoons salt
½ teaspoon pepper
6 large carrots
1 pound string beans
½ pound yellow turnips
4 tablespoons enriched flour
4 tablespoons water

Peel vegetables and cut into match-like pieces.* Brown green pepper and scallions in margarine over low heat. Add bouillon cubes and boiling water. Stir until cubes are dissolved. Add celery leaves, seasonings and vegetables. Bring to a boil and cook, covered, 10 minutes. Make a paste of the flour and cold water; add to stew and mix thoroughly. Add dumplings as directed in Nutmeg Dumplings recipe. Yield: 6 servings.

**julienne strips*

Nutmeg Dumplings

2 tablespoons margarine
6 large potatoes, cooked
½ teaspoon salt
1 teaspoon nutmeg
2 tablespoons enriched flour
2 tablespoons bread crumbs
4 eggs, beaten

Mash potatoes. Mix with margarine, seasonings, flour, crumbs and eggs. Beat thoroughly. Drop by tablespoons into boiling vegetables. Cover and cook 12 to 15 minutes. Yields: 2 dozen dumplings.

Modern variation: Vegetable stock can be used in place of bouillon and water.

WILTED LETTUCE

4 slices cut up bacon
¼ cup vinegar
2 tablespoon water
1 quart shredded lettuce
2 chopped green onions
2 teaspoons sugar

Fry bacon until crisp. Add vinegar and water and heat. Add lettuce and green onions. Season with salt and pepper and sugar. Toss until wilted. Serves 6.

HONEY-GLAZED CARROTS

2 tablespoons honey
2 tablespoons margarine
1 teaspoon grated orange rind
¼ teaspoon salt
6 cooked carrots, sliced

Combine honey, margarine, orange rind and salt. Bring to boil. Add sliced carrots and simmer 10 minutes. Serves 4.

CORN PUDDING

3 eggs
2 cups fresh or canned corn
2 tablespoons melted margarine
salt and pepper
2 cups milk

Beat the eggs. Add all the other ingredients and salt and pepper to taste. Pour into a greased baking dish, place in a pan of hot water, and bake in a moderate oven for about 1 hour or until set in the center. Yields 6 servings.

LIMAS AU PUFF

3 cups lima beans
1 cup sliced onions
1 tablespoon cornstarch
1/2 teaspoon salt
1/4 teaspoon pepper
1/3 cup mayonnaise
1 egg white, stiffly beaten

Cook limas in boiling salted water until tender. Add onions last 15 minutes of cooking. Drain. Place in greased casserole. Mix 1 cup of vegetable liquid with cornstarch and seasonings. Cook, stirring constantly until thickened. Pour over vegetables in casserole. Fold mayonnaise into egg white. Spread on top of casserole. Bake in hot over (425°F) 10 minutes. Top with strips of broiled bacon, if desired. Yield: 6 servings.

HARVARD BEETS

1 tablespoon cornstarch, or 2 tablespoons flour
½ cup sugar
½ teaspoon salt
½ cup vinegar
3 tablespoons margarine
3 cups cooked beets, sliced

Mix the cornstarch flour, sugar, and salt. Add the vinegar and boil 5 minutes, stirring constantly. Add the margarine and beets, and let stand until the sauce becomes red. Reheat if necessary. The acid of the vinegar brings out the bright red color. Yields 6 servings.

ZIPPY BEETS

2 1/2 cups cooked beets
1/3 cup top milk*
2 1/2 tablespoons horseradish
1 teaspoon salt

Cut cooked beets into long strips. Heat with top milk, horseradish and salt. Toss lightly to mix well. Makes 6 servings.

**Top milk refers to the upper layer of milk in the container enriched by whatever cream has risen to the top. Half and Half can be used as a substitute.*

SPRING FANCY

2 cups slivered carrots
2 cups slivered, pared potatoes
4 tablespoons butter
1/8 teaspoon pepper
1/2 cup minced parsley

Cook carrots and potatoes in boiling water for 10 minutes. Drain. Toss lightly with butter, pepper and parsley. Makes 4 servings.

VICTORY PANCAKES

1/2 medium onion
2 medium potatoes
3 carrots
2 cups fresh spinach
1/4 head lettuce
2 eggs, well beaten
1 cup flour
1 teaspoon baking powder
1 1/2 teaspoons salt
1/8 teaspoon pepper

Chop onion, potatoes, carrots and lettuce in food chopper using a fine blade. Save juice.* Blend in eggs. Sift flour, baking powder and salt, and sift into vegetables. Mix well. Drop by spoonfuls into hot fat in skillet. Fry on both sides until golden brown. Makes 12 pancakes. Serve plain or with cheese sauce.

**To use in other recipes*

DEVILED STRING BEANS

3 tablespoons margarine
1½ pounds string beans
1 small onion
1 tablespoon prepared mustard with horseradish

Cook string beans and onion together in boiling, salted water until tender. Drain. Cream margarine and mustard together and add to beans. Mix well. Garnish with parsley. Yield: 6 servings.

EGGPLANT SANDWICHES

¼ lb American cheese
1 eggplant, small
1 egg, beaten
1½ cups crushed Wheaties
salt and pepper

Slice cheese thin. Slice eggplant into ¼-inch thick slices. Place a slice of cheese, sprinkled with salt and pepper, between each 2 pieces of eggplant. Dip sandwiches into beaten egg and crushed Wheaties. Brown slowly in hot fat. Makes 5 servings.

FIVE-MINUTE CABBAGE

Heat 3 cups of milk, add 2 quarts of shredded cabbage, and simmer for about 2 minutes. Mix 3 tablespoons of flour with 3 tablespoons of melted margarine. Add to this blended flour and margarine a little of the hot milk. Stir into the cabbage and cook for 3 or 4 minutes, stirring all the while. Season to taste with salt and pepper and serve at once. Yields 6 servings.

WESTERN BEANS

Brown a chopped onion in 2 tablespoons of margarine. Add 2 cups of cooked tomatoes seasoned with salt and pepper. Bring to a boil and add 1 quart of cooked beans. Simmer 15 to 20 minutes. Sprinkle with parsley and serve hot. Yields 6 servings.

BROCCOLI WITH HOLLANDAISE SAUCE

½ cup margarine
4 egg yolks
¼ cup water
2 tablespoons lemon juice
salt, pepper
cooked broccoli

Put all ingredients, except broccoli, in the top of a double boiler or a small deep saucepan. Put over direct heat, and beat constantly with a dover beater,* until the sauce is thick, smooth and foamy.

Serve on hot cooked broccoli, or other cooked green vegetables.

* *A dover beater is another term for an egg beater.*

NUTBURGERS

1½ cups ground pecans (2 cups whole pecans)
1 cup soft bread crumbs, (packed in cup)
1 egg, well beaten
1 teaspoon finely chopped onion
1 tablespoon finely cut parsley
1½ teaspoons salt
1 cup milk

Mix all ingredients thoroughly. Chill 2 hours. Drop spoonfuls into hot greased skillet, brown 5 minutes on each side. (Nuts burn easily.) Serve with Hot Mushroom Sauce.

Hot Mushroom Sauce: ½ lb sautéed mushrooms in 1½ cups Thick White Sauce—with 1 tablespoon cooking sherry.

SCOTCH-IRISH POTATOES

4 cold, boiled potatoes
1 egg, or
¼ cup undiluted evaporated milk
salt
pepper
onion juice*
quick oats
margarine

Peel and cut potatoes into ¼-inch slices. Dip in egg or milk and sprinkle with salt, pepper, and onion juice. Dip in oats. Brown slowly in margarine and serve hot.

* *To make onion juice roughly chop a medium onion into small to medium sized pieces. Drop into a blender and blend at medium speed for about one minute, or until you have a fine puree. Place a strainer over a bowl, and place a piece of cheesecloth into the strainer. Pour the blended onion into the cheesecloth, and press through the strainer into the bowl with a spoon or rubber spatula.*

MAYONNAISE CURRY SAUCE

2 tablespoons real mayonnaise
1 large onion, sliced
3 tablespoons enriched all-purpose flour
¼ teaspoon pepper
½ teaspoon curry powder
1 bouillon cube
1½ cups boiling water
cooked rice
pimento, if desired

Sauté onion in mayonnaise over low heat. Add flour and seasonings and stir until smooth. Dissolve bouillon cube in boiling water. Add bouillon water gradually to onion mixture. Cook, stirring constantly, until smooth and thickened. Serve with rice, garnished with pimento. Yield: 6 servings.

V-mail Poster. United States Government Printing Office. Circa 1943.

Other WW 2 Home Front History — V-Mail

Whether wartime or peacetime, service people and their loved ones at home want to keep in touch as much as they can. During WW2, the government devised a special way for families in the United States to write to their loved ones overseas. It was called V-Mail, and the "V" stood for "victory." The word "Victory" was probably one of the most popular words in the lexicon of the time. It appeared everywhere; in advertising, product names, even in the names of some ration recipes.

V-Mail packets could be purchased at a dime store or at the Post Office. Inside the packet were sheets of writing paper where a letter could be typed or written with black ink onto a printed form. Printed on the back of the sheet was an envelope form. Once finished, the letter was folded, following the enveloped form, sealed and addressed, and dropped into a mailbox. But before being sent overseas, it would be opened and read by military censors to insure that it did not contain information that could compromise national security in the event it should fall into enemy hands.

After the military read the letters they were then microfilmed onto a large reel, which contained hundreds of letters, and sent overseas. Once the reels arrived at their destination, they were printed out in a smaller size and sent on to the serviceman or woman they were addressed to. This process saved valuable space on cargo planes because a single reel of microfilm could take the place of as many as 20 sacks of letters.

"It was patriotic to write V-mail letters. Virtually every young man in our town had gone to fight the war. You had a feeling of being in contact. It gave you a sense of community."

— Dr. Tom Barrett

20 UNITED STATES OF AMERICA 20
OFFICE OF PRICE ADMINISTRATION
RATION COUPON
FOR
TWENTY
POINTS
MEAT, FATS, FISH, and CHEESES
20 OPA Form R-1615 20

CHAPTER SEVEN

BREADS AND PASTRIES

20 UNITED STATES OF AMERICA 20
OFFICE OF PRICE ADMINISTRATION
RATION COUPON
FOR
TWENTY
POINTS
PROCESSED FOODS
20 OPA Form R-1325 20

During the 1940s, many families still baked their own bread, and piecrusts were always made from scratch. There were also three different classifications of baking powder; tartrate, phosphate, and double-acting. Today we use double-acting baking powder. However, for historic purposes, the older references to baking powders have been left in some of the recipes that follow. Most, if not all, of the pie recipes could also be made using modern, pre-made frozen piecrusts.

Bottled water is recommended for those recipes using yeast, as chlorinated tap water can kill the yeast.

Bread Baking Poster. United States Government Printing Office. Circa 1943.

FRESH-YEAST BREAD

2 cups (1 pint) milk, scalded*
4 tablespoons sugar, or 3 tablespoons strained honey
1½ tablespoons salt
3 tablespoons shortening
1 cake compressed yeast or 1 package granular yeast**
2 cups (1 pint) warm water
12 cups (3 lbs) sifted enriched flour

Combine milk, sugar, salt and shortening, stirring until dissolved. Cool to lukewarm. Soften yeast in a small amount of the water. Add yeast and remaining water to the cooled milk mixture. Sift flour once, measure, and add to yeast mixture, blending thoroughly.

Knead dough on a floured board. To do this: flatten dough, then fold edge of dough toward you. Push dough away from you with palms of hands. Turn dough around slightly and repeat folding and pressing. If dough sticks, add a little flour to molding board. To obtain a fine grain, kneading should continue for 10 minutes. Place dough in a greased bowl; cover and allow to rise in a warm place (80° to 85°F) about 2 hours, or until dough maintains the impression of a finger.

Punch gas from dough by plunging the fist in center of dough. Fold over edges of dough; turn upside down. Place in the center of board and allow to rise in a warm place about ½ hour.

Remove dough to floured board and flatten out. Divide into 4 pieces; mold into balls; allow to stand, tightly covered, for 15 minutes. Shape into loaves.

Place in greased 8½ x 4 x 3-inch bread pans and cover. Allow to stand in warm place until dough fills the pan and center is well about top of pan (about 2 hours). Bake in hot oven (400°F) about 40 minutes. Do not store until cold. Yields 4 1-lb loaves.

**Scalding milk was used before the process of pasteurization. This step is no longer necessary.*

*** A cake of yeast is equal to one package of dry yeast or 1 scant tablespoon.*

HALF AND HALF WHEAT BREAD

3 1/2 cups sifted enriched flour
3 cups un-sifted whole wheat of graham flour
1 cup milk, scalded*
1 cake compressed yeast, or 1 package granular yeast**
1 cup lukewarm water
1/3 cup molasses or strained honey
3 teaspoons salt
2 tablespoons shortening

Sift flour once, measure; add whole wheat flour; mix well.

Cool milk to lukewarm. Soften yeast in small amount of water. Add with remaining water to milk. Add molasses or honey, salt and shortening. Add flour and work in thoroughly. Knead on floured board until smooth, about 10 minutes. Let rise in warm place until doubled in bulk, about 2½ hours.

Punch dough down, let rise again in warm place for about ½ hour.

Divide dough into two equal parts and mold into balls; allow to stand closely covered for 15 minutes. Shape into loaves. Place in greased bread pans, 8½ x 4½ inches, cover and allow to stand until dough comes well about top of pans, about 1 ½ to 2 hours.

Bake at 400ºF for about 40 minutes. Do not store until cold. Makes 2 loaves.

**Scalding milk was used before the process of pasteurization. This step is no longer necessary.*

*** One package of dry yeast is one scant tablespoon.*

DRY-YEAST BREAD

Yeast Ferment: Prepare the afternoon before baking

1 cake dry yeast*
½ cup lukewarm water**
1 cup mashed potato
1 tablespoon sugar
2 cups (1 pint) potato water
1½ cups lukewarm water

Break yeast into ½ cup lukewarm water. Combine potato, sugar, potato water, and softened yeast. Blend well. Add remaining water (1 cup); cover; set aside in warm place (80ºF) until next morning.

Dough:

4 teaspoons salt
4 tablespoons sugar
4 tablespoons shortening, melted
12 cups (3 lbs) sifted enriched flour

In the morning add salt, sugar, and shortening to yeast ferment; mix well. Add about 1/3 of the flour; beat well. Add remaining flour to make a soft dough. Knead dough on a floured board. To do this: flatten dough, then fold edge of dough toward you. Push dough away from you with palms of hands. Turn dough around slightly and repeat folding and pressing. If dough sticks, add a little flour to molding board. To obtain a fine grain, kneading should continue for 10 minutes. Place dough in a greased bowl; cover and allow to rise in a warm place (80º to 85ºF) about 2 hours, or until dough maintains the impression of a finger when pressed into the dough.

Punch gas from dough by plunging the fist in center of dough. Fold over edges of dough; turn upside down. Center on board and allow to rise in a warm place about ½ hour.

Remove dough to floured board and flatten out. Divide into 4 pieces; mold into balls; allow balls to stand, closely covered, for 15 minutes. Shape into loaves.

Place in greased 8½ x 4 x 3-inch bread pans and cover. Allow to stand in warm place until dough fills the pan and center is well about top of pan (about 2 hours). Bake in hot oven (400°F) about 40 minutes. Do not store until cold. Yields 4 1-lb. loaves.

* *A cake of yeast is equal to one package of dry yeast or 1 scant tablespoon.*

** *For best results, dissolve yeast in bottled water.*

OATMEAL BREAD

2 cups rolled or quick oatmeal
$2^3/4$ cups water
2 teaspoon salt
1 tablespoon shortening
1 cake compressed yeast*
1 teaspoon sugar
$^1/3$ cup brown sugar
$4^1/2$ cups sifted flour

Stir oatmeal into 2 cups boiling water and salt. Add shortening. Stir until smooth. Cool to lukewarm. (About 1 hour.) Crumble yeast into bowl. Add ¼ cup warm water** and sugar. Combine with lukewarm oatmeal mixture. Work in flour. Knead until smooth. Place in greased bowl. Cover with damp cloth. Let rise until double (1½ hours). Punch down. (Dough gets sticky; for easy handling, knead in about ½ cup flour.) Divide in half. Place in 2 greased bread loaf pans. Shape with hands to form loaves. Let rise until almost double (1¼ hours.) Bake 15 minutes in hot oven (425°F), then about 30 minutes in quick moderate oven (375°F). Makes two 1 lb loaves.

* *A cake of yeast is equal to one package of dry yeast or 1 scant tablespoon.*

** *For best results, dissolve yeast in bottled water.*

WHOLE WHEAT ROLLS

1 cake compressed yeast*
1¾ cups lukewarm milk
2 tablespoons sugar
1 tablespoon salt
2 tablespoons molasses
2 cups flour, sifted
3 cups medium whole wheat flour
4 tablespoons soft shortening

Crumble yeast into bowl. Add lukewarm milk, sugar, salt, and molasses. Work in sifted flour, whole wheat flour, and shortening. Knead until smooth. Place in greased bowl. Cover with damp cloth. Let rise until double (2 hours.) Punch down. Let rise until almost double (45 minutes.) Punch down. Let rest 15 minutes. Shape. Place in greased pan. Let rise. (30 to 40 minutes.) Bake 15 to 20 minutes (depending on size) in hot oven (425ºF). Makes 2 dozen rolls.

** A cake of yeast is equal to one package of dry yeast or 1 scant tablespoon.*

SPOON BREAD

Into a soup kettle put the following:
1 pint milk
1 teaspoon salt
$^{2}/3$ cup cornmeal
1 tablespoon sugar
2 tablespoon margarine
3 eggs
2 teaspoons baking powder

Place over the fire and let cook until a stiff mush, stirring often to prevent lumping. Remove from fire and stir until it cools. Break three eggs, one at a time, into the mush and beat very hard after each addition. Then add two teaspoons baking powder. Put in margarine-greased casserole, or deep pie pan, and bake in moderate oven (375°F) for 30 to 40 minutes. Serve from pan in which it is baked. Plenty of margarine should be served with spoon bread. Serves 4 to 6.

REFRIGERATOR ROLLS

¾ cups milk, scalded*
¼ cup sugar, or 3 tablespoons strained honey
3 tablespoons shortening
1 teaspoon salt
1 cake compressed yeast, or 1 package granular yeast
¼ cup lukewarm water
1 egg, slightly beaten
3½ cups sifted enriched flour

Pour milk over sugar, shortening, and salt in mixing bowl. Cool to lukewarm.

Soften yeast in lukewarm water;** add egg and mix well; add to milk mixture.

Sift flour once, measure; add about half to yeast mixture and beat thoroughly. Add remaining flour; mix well. Place dough in greased bowl; cover, and let rise in warm place for about 1 hour. Punch down, grease top of dough lightly; cover bowl with a slightly dampened towel and waxed paper; tie securely. Store in refrigerator or cold place until needed.

About 2½ hours before baking, take from refrigerator amount of dough needed. Shape as desired. Cover and let rise until double in bulk (about 2 hours). Bake in hot oven (425°F) for about 20 minutes.

Modern variation: Milk and water can be made lukewarm by cooking in the microwave for about 30 seconds.

**Scalding was used before the process of pasteurization. This step is no longer necessary.*

*** For best results, dissolve yeast in bottled water.*

NUT QUICK BREAD

4 cups sifted enriched flour
6 teaspoons baking powder (or 4 teaspoons double-acting)*
3 teaspoons salt
½ cup sugar
1 cup chopped walnuts
2 cups milk
2 eggs, slightly beaten
4 tablespoons shortening, melted

Sift flour once, measure; add baking powder, salt and sugar; sift together twice. Add nutmeats; mix well. Combine milk and eggs; add to dry ingredients. Add shortening, mixing only until all flour is dampened. Turn into well-greased loaf pan, filling 2/3 full. Push batter well up corners of the pan, leaving center slightly hollowed. Bake in moderate oven (350°F) until done, about 1 hour, 15 minutes for a large loaf, about 1 hour for smaller loaves. Brush top with melted butter, if desired. Remove from pan; cool completely on cooling rack before serving. This bread slices better on the second day. Makes one 9 x 3 x 3-inch loaf or two 8 x 4 x 2 loaves.

Note: If desired, 6 tablespoons strained honey may be substituted for sugar. Add with combined milk and egg.

QUICK CELERY CRESCENTS

1½ cups milk
2 tablespoon sugar
1 teaspoon salt
6 tablespoons shortening
2 cakes compressed yeast
4 cups sifted flour
celery seeds

Heat milk, sugar, salt and shortening. Cool to lukewarm, then crumble and add yeast. Beat in sifted flour, 2 cups at a time. Place in greased bowl. Cover with damp cloth. Let rise until double (about 30 minutes.) Punch down. Divide in half. Roll each into a circle (12 inches in diameter, ¼-inch thick.) Brush with melted butter. Cut into 12 pie-shaped pieces.

Beginning at wide end, roll up·each piece tightly. Pull ends to make longer and form into crescent. Place (with point down) on greased baking sheet. Brush with melted butter, sprinkle with celery seeds and salt. Let rise until double (15 minutes). Bake 12 to15 minutes in hot oven (450°F). Yield: 2 dozen rolls.

PLAIN PANCAKES

2 cups cold milk (or half water)
2 cups pancake flour

Add liquid to flour, beating until smooth. Bake on hot, lightly greased griddle; turning only once. Makes about 10 to 12, 4 ½-inch pancakes.

For economy: Substitute water for milk, increasing flour to 2¼ cups.

For richer pancakes: Add 2 tablespoons melted shortening or decrease milk to 1¾ cups and add 1egg, well beaten, to liquid.

BUCKWHEAT PANCAKES

2½ cups cold milk
2 cups buckwheat pancake flour

Add milk to flour, beating until smooth. Bake on hot, lightly greased griddle, turning only once. For thinner pancakes, use more liquid; for thicker pancakes use more flour. Makes about fourteen 4½-inch pancakes.

For economy: Substitute 2¼ cups water for milk.

For richer pancakes: Add 2 tablespoons melted shortening to recipe or decrease milk to 2¼ cups and combine with 1 egg, well beaten.

CRISP WAFFLES

2 cups sifted flour
2 teaspoons baking powder
½ teaspoon salt
2 egg yolks, well beaten
1 cup milk
¼ cup melted shortening

Sift flour once, measure, add baking powder and salt, and sift again. Combine egg yolks, milk, and shortening; add to flour, beating until smooth. Beat egg whites until they hold up in moist peaks. Stir quickly but thoroughly into batter. Bake in hot waffle iron. Bakes four, 4-section waffles.

Waffle Variations:

Sprinkle about 3 tablespoons chopped almonds, walnuts, or pecan nutmeats in waffle iron before pouring in batter.

Sprinkle about 3 tablespoons grated strong cheese* over waffles before baking.

**Strong Cheese is any cheese you like that has a bite to it, such as; feta or sharp cheddar. The technique for creating a real strong cheese is to cut off the dried rinds and ends of any hunk of cheese and put it into cool, dry place to ferment, usually a wooden box in a cool dry place. After a time, the cheese will mold and dry. Once the cheese is dry and moldy remove the moldy parts and cover the remaining cheese with a wine or soup broth and let sit for a couple of days until the cheese rinds soften again. Once softened mash all the rinds together to create 'strong cheese.'*

CRISPY CORN MEAL WAFFLES

3/4 cup sifted cake flour
1 1/4 cup yellow corn meal
2 1/2 teaspoons baking powder
3/4 teaspoon salt
2 eggs, separated
1 cup milk
1/3 cup melted margarine, cooled slightly

Sift flour. Measure. Sift again with corn meal, baking powder and salt. Mix well. Beat egg whites until stiff but not dry; set aside. Beat egg yolks and add milk and margarine. Add to flour mixture, beating until smooth. Fold in egg whites. Bake in moderately hot waffle iron about 6 minutes or until done. If batter thickens on standing, add more milk, a tablespoonful at a time. Yields 4, four-section waffles.

CORN STICKS

1 cup corn meal
½ cup flour
½ teaspoon salt
¼ teaspoon soda
½ cup buttermilk
1 egg
½ teaspoon melted margarine

Sift corn meal, flour, salt, soda three times. Add the buttermilk and beaten egg yolk, melted margarine, and lastly beaten egg white. Pour small amount into piping hot, greased corn stick pans and bake in hot oven (425°F) for 15 minutes. Serve hot and with a generous amount of margarine.

BUTTERMILK BISCUITS

2 cups flour
½ teaspoon baking soda
½ teaspoon salt
1 tablespoon baking powder
2 tablespoons margarine
¾ cup sour milk or buttermilk

Mix and sift dry ingredients. Work in margarine with a fork, add the sour milk gradually to make soft dough. Roll to ½-inch thick, cut, place on baking sheet; bake in moderately hot oven, (400°F) until done and brown. Yields 16 biscuits.

Modern adaptation: To turn plain milk into buttermilk simply place a scant tablespoon of white vinegar or lemon juice in a measuring cup and fill with milk until it reaches the ¾ mark. Let it sit for 5 minutes before using. Prepare as directed above. Bake for approximately 15 to 20 minutes. Yield will vary, depending on the size of the biscuit cutter used.

WARTIME DROP BISCUITS

2 cups sifted cake flour
2½ teaspoons baking powder
¾ teaspoon salt
¾ cup milk
1 tablespoon melted shortening or oil

Sift flour once, measure, add baking powder and salt, and sift again. Add milk and melted shortening. Then stir quickly and lightly until all flour is dampened. Drop from tip of teaspoon in small amounts on lightly greased baking sheet. Bake in hot oven (430°F) 15 minutes, or until done. Makes about 18 biscuits.

HONEY NUT BISCUITS

$^{1}/_{3}$ cup chopped nuts
$^{1}/_{3}$ cup honey
2 tablespoons melted margarine
2 cups flour
4 teaspoons baking powder
1 teaspoon salt
4 tablespoons margarine
$^{3}/_{4}$ cup milk

Mix nuts, honey and melted margarine; place in muffin pans. Sift together flour, baking powder and salt. Cut in margarine. Stir in milk. Drop dough in muffin pans. Bake in hot oven (425°F) 12-15 minutes. Turn out while hot. Makes 10 delicious biscuits.

B1 BISCUITS

1½ cups enriched all-purpose flour
½ teaspoon salt
2½ teaspoons baking powder
½ cups oats
1 tablespoon sugar
2 tablespoons margarine
3 tablespoons peanut butter
1 cup milk

Sift and measure flour. Resift with salt and baking powder. Stir in oats and sugar. Cut in margarine and peanut butter and add milk. Mix very lightly. Fill well-greased muffin pans ½ full. Brush tops with milk. Bake at 450°F for 20-25 minutes. Yield: 12 biscuits.

SAVORY BISCUITS FOR MEAT PIES

Use ½ recipe Wartime Drop Biscuits (page 153) or Low-Shortening Biscuits (below). Mix as directed, sifting one of the following seasoning with the flour: ¾ teaspoon curry powder, ½ teaspoon celery seed, or ¼ teaspoon poultry seasoning. Drop biscuits or place rolled biscuits on hot stew or creamed mixture. Bake in hot oven (425°F) 25 minutes, or until biscuits are done.

LOW-SHORTENING BISCUITS

2 cups sifted flour
2½ teaspoons baking powder
¼ teaspoon salt
2 tablespoons cold shortening
½ cup plus 1 teaspoon milk

Sift flour once, measure, add baking powder and salt, and sift again. Cut shortening into small pieces and add to flour. Cut in shortening, using pastry blender or finger tips, until mixture is as fine as meal.

Add milk all at once and stir carefully until all flour is dampened. Then stir quickly and lightly until mixture forms a soft dough and follows spoon around bowl. Turn out on lightly floured board and knead gently 15 times. Roll 3/8-inch thick. Cut with floured 1¾-inch biscuit cutter. Bake on lightly greased sheet in hot oven (450°F) about 15 minutes. Do not over- or under-bake these biscuits. Makes 16 biscuits.

Note: for tall, soft biscuits, place close together on baking sheet; for biscuits with crusted edges, place slightly apart.

CROSS BAR TEA BISCUITS

2 cups sifted enriched flour
3 tablespoons baking powder (or 1½ tablespoons double-acting)*
¼ teaspoon salt
¼ cup shortening
¾ cup milk

Sift flour once, measure, add baking powder and salt, and sift together. Cut in shortening with a pastry blender or two knives until mixture resembles coarse meal. Make a well in center of flour mixture; add milk all at once. Mix with a fork or spatula until all flour is dampened. Turn on a floured board; knead lightly for a few seconds to form a smooth dough. Pat or roll dough to about ½-inch thickness. Cut into strips 2 x ½ inches. Place two strips crosswise in each greased muffin pan. Combine 2 tablespoons melted butter and ½ cup honey or corn syrup; drip over tops of biscuits. Bake in hot oven (450°F) for about 12 to 15 minutes. Remove from pans immediately. Makes 12 to 14.

**Most modern baking powders are double-acting.*

LOW-SHORTENING MUFFINS

1½ cups sifted flour
2 teaspoons baking powder
½ teaspoon salt
2 tablespoons sugar
1 egg, beaten
½ cup milk
1 tablespoon melted shortening or oil

Sift flour once, measure, add baking powder, salt, and sugar, and sift again. Add egg, milk, and shortening. Stir only enough to dampen all flour. Bake in greased muffin pans, in hot oven (425°F) for about 22 minutes for large muffins, 15 minutes for medium muffins. Makes 8 to 12 muffins.

SPICED APPLE MUFFINS

Mix muffins as directed in the Low-Shortening Muffins above, adding ½ cup chopped, sliced apples with the egg, milk and shortening. Mix and turn into greased muffin pans. Sprinkle top with mixture of 2 tablespoons sugar, ⅛ teaspoon cinnamon, and dash of nutmeg. Bake as above, allowing 20 to 25 minutes.

JELLY SURPRISE MUFFINS

1 2/3 cups sifted enriched flour
2 1/2 teaspoons baking powder (or 1¾ teaspoons double-acting)*
1/2 teaspoon salt
1/4 cup sugar
1 egg, well beaten
3/4 cup milk
4 tablespoons shortening, melted
tart jelly

Sift flour once, measure; add baking powder, salt, and sugar, sift again. Add combined egg and milk; add shortening, mixing only until all flour is dampened. Fill greased, medium-sized muffin pans about ¼ full; place about ½ teaspoon jelly on each, top with remaining batter. Do not fill pans more than 2/3 full. Bake in hot oven (425°F) about 20 to 25 minutes until brown. Makes about 10 to 12 medium muffins.

Note: If desired, substitute 3 tablespoons light corn syrup for sugar. Add with combined egg and milk.

* *Most modern baking powders are double-acting.*

MAYONNAISE MUFFINS

3 tablespoons mayonnaise
2 cups sifted enriched flour
3 teaspoons baking powder
½ teaspoon salt
3 tablespoons sugar
1 egg, well beaten
1 cup milk

Sift flour, baking powder, salt, and sugar together three times. Combine egg and milk. Add to flour mixture. Add mayonnaise and mix well. Fill greased muffin pans 2/3 full. Bake in hot oven (425°F) 20 - 30 minutes. Yield: 1 dozen muffins.

QUICK YEAST MUFFINS

1 cake compressed yeast
¼ cup lukewarm water (for best results used bottled water)
5 tablespoons sugar
½ cup lukewarm milk
3 cups flour, sifted
½ cup shortening, melted
1 egg, well beaten

Crumble yeast into bowl. Add lukewarm water, 1 tablespoon sugar and stir in lukewarm milk. Beat in 1 cup sifted flour. Let rise 30 minutes. Mix in melted shortening, egg, salt, 4 tablespoons sugar, 2 cups sifted flour. Fill greased muffin cups ½ full. Let rise 20 to 30 minutes. Bake 25 minutes in quick moderate oven (375°F). Yield: 12 medium-sized muffins.

RAISIN COFFEE CAKE

2 cups sifted cake flour
2½ teaspoons baking powder
¾ teaspoon salt
2 tablespoons sugar
2 tablespoons cold shortening
¼ cup chopped raisins
½ teaspoon grated orange rind
1 egg, well beaten
½ cup milk
2½ tablespoons sugar
¼ teaspoon cinnamon
¼ teaspoon nutmeg

Sift flour once, measure, add baking powder, salt and sugar, and sift again. Cut shortening in small pieces and add to flour. Cut in shortening, using a pastry blender or finger tips, until mixture is as fine as meal. Add raisins and orange rind. Combine egg and milk, add to flour, then stir only until all flour is dampened. Spread in greased 8 x 8 x 2-inch pan. Mix sugar and spices together and sprinkle over batter. Bake in hot oven (425°F) 16 minutes.

QUICK CINNAMON COFFEE CAKE

2 cups sifted flour
½ teaspoon salt
4 tablespoons sugar
4 teaspoons baking powder
1 egg, well beaten
1 cup milk
4 tablespoons shortening, melted
½ teaspoon cinnamon

Sift together flour, salt, 2 tablespoons sugar and baking powder. Stir in egg and milk. Add melted shortening. Spread in greased 8-inch square pan. Sprinkle with 2 tablespoons sugar and cinnamon. Bake about 30 minutes in quick moderate oven (375°F). Serve warm as bread or dessert.

QUICK APPLE COFFEE CAKE

Spread Quick Cinnamon Coffee Cake batter in 8-inch square pan. Press 1/8-inch thick apple slices into top in rows. Sprinkle with sugar and cinnamon or drip 4 tablespoons raspberry jam or other jam over apples. Bake about 30 minutes in quick moderate oven (375°F).

FRUIT SCONES

2 cups sifted enriched flour
3 teaspoons baking powder (or 2 teaspoons double-acting)*
½ teaspoon salt
¼ cup shortening
1½ teaspoons grated orange rind
½ cup seedless raisins, dates, currants, etc.
2 eggs, slightly beaten
¼ cup milk
2 tablespoons strained honey

Sift flour once, measure; add baking powder and salt; sift together twice. Cut in shortening with a pastry blender or two knives until mixture resembles coarse meal. Add orange rind and fruit. Make a well in center; add combined eggs, milk and honey all at once. Mix with a spoon until all the flour is dampened. Turn out on a floured board; knead lightly to smooth surface. Divide dough into four equal parts; shape each into a round ball. Pat or roll each quarter into circle about ½-inch thick. Cut through centers with well-floured knife into 6 scones. Place on greased baking sheet. Brush top lightly with milk; sprinkle with sugar. Bake in hot oven (425°F) for about 15 minutes. Serve warm. Makes 2 dozen scones.

**Most modern baking powders are double-acting.*

FRUIT ROLL

1½ cups light corn syrup
½ cup water
1 tablespoon butter
½ teaspoon cinnamon
2 cups freshly cut fruit (apples, rhubarb, strawberries, etc.)
Bisquick

Heat corn syrup and water to boiling in 8-inch square pan. Make rich Bisquick dough (see recipe on side of Bisquick package.) Roll out dough, ½-inch thick, 6 x12 inches, oblong. Spread with cut fruit, dot with butter, sprinkle with cinnamon. Roll up, seal well. Cut into slices (1 to 1½ inches.) Quickly place slices (cut side down) in pan of boiling syrup. Bake immediately, about 25 minutes, in hot oven (450°F). Makes 10 servings.

APPLE OR PEACH DUMPLINGS

2 tablespoons shortening
1 cup Bisquick
1 to 2 tablespoons water
4 cored or pitted fresh fruit
1 tablespoon jam

Cut shortening into Bisquick. Blend in water. Roll into 12-inch square. Cut into 4 6-inch squares. Place fruit on each square. Fill hollow with jam. Wrap pastry around fruit. Seal well. Bake 20 to 25 minutes in hot oven (450°F). Makes 4 servings.

Modern adaptation: If using fresh apples decrease amount of fruit to 1 or 2 apples. If dough is too dry and crumbly add small amounts of water or milk. The biscuit recipe on the side of the Bisquick box can also be used.

APPLE TEA RING

3 tablespoons sugar
¾ teaspoon salt
3 tablespoons shortening
¾ cup milk, scalded*
1 cake compressed yeast or 1 package granulated yeast
1 egg, well beaten
2¾ cups sifted enriched flour
1 tablespoon melted butter
3 tablespoons sugar
1 teaspoon cinnamon
3 tablespoons chopped walnuts or nutmeats
1 cup diced apples

Add sugar, salt, and shortening to milk; cool to lukewarm. Soften yeast in small amount of lukewarm milk. Add to milk mixture. Add egg.

Sift flour once; measure. Add to yeast mixture in about two portions, mixing well to make a soft dough. Knead or beat in the bowl for about 5 minutes. Place in greased bowl; cover and allow to rise in a warm place (80°F) until double in bulk (about 1½ hours). Roll out into a rectangle 12 x 10 inches. Brush with melted butter. Combine last four ingredients; spread over dough. Roll up as for jelly roll, the long way of the dough. Place on a greased baking sheet and bring ends together to form a ring, sealing ends securely. Make slits in the ring with scissors about one inch apart, cutting about ¼ of the way to center of ring. Turn each piece on its side, showing cut ridge up. Cover and let rise until double in bulk (about 1 ¼ hours). Bake in moderate oven (375°F) about 30 minutes until done. Serve warm, plain; or with butter.

Note: If desired, omit sugar in dough. Add 2 tablespoons light corn syrup. Increase salt to 1 teaspoon.

**Scalding milk is no longer necessary in modern baking as the milk we buy today is pasteurized. Heat milk to a low temperature to soften the yeast.*

DATE NUT SANDWICH LOAF

2 cups flour
2½ teaspoons baking powder
¾ teaspoon salt
4 tablespoons sugar
½ cup chopped dates
½ cup chopped nut meats
2 teaspoons grated orange rind
1 egg, beaten
1 cup milk

Sift flour once, measure, add baking powder, salt, and sugar, and sift again. Add dates, nuts, and orange rind, and mix carefully. Add egg and milk, stir until blended. Turn into greased loaf pan, 8 x 4 x 3 inches. Bake in a moderate oven (350°F) 1 hour and 20 minutes, or until done. Store overnight before slicing.

LEMON SHORTCAKES

2 cups sifted flour
3 teaspoons baking powder
2 tablespoons sugar
1 teaspoon salt
1 teaspoon grated lemon rind
6 tablespoons margarine
2/3 cup milk (about)
1 tablespoon melted margarine
fresh or canned fruit
dash of mace*, if desired

Sift flour. Measure. Add baking powder, sugar, and salt and sift again into a bowl. Add grated lemon rind and mace. Cut in margarine with a pastry blender or two knives, blending until mixture resembles coarse corn meal. Add milk, stirring until flour is dampened. Turn out on lightly floured board; knead 30 seconds. Roll dough about ¼-inch thick; cut with large biscuit cutter or floured knife. Put half of shortcakes on greased baking sheet. Brush tops with melted margarine. Bake in hot oven (450°F) 12 to 15 minutes. Split and serve with any fresh or canned fruit and cream, if desired. Makes about 8 shortcakes.

**Mace is another name for nutmeg.*

TOP-CRUST PIE OR COBBLER

6 to 8 apples, thinly sliced (about 6 cups)
2/3 cup sugar
1/8 teaspoon salt
3/4 teaspoon cinnamon
1/4 teaspoon nutmeg
2 tablespoons lemon juice
1/4 teaspoon lemon rind
1 recipe Victory Pie Crust *

Combine apples, sugar, salt, lemon juice, and rind. Turn into pie plate, 8 x 8 x 2-inch pan, or individual baking dishes. (Fresh cherries or other fruit may also be used.)

Prepare pastry, using 4 tablespoons shortening and 3 tablespoons ice water. Place on lightly floured board; shape and roll to fit pan. For individual baking dishes roll pastry 1/8-inch thick and cut circles to fit. Fit pastry over apples and press against pan. Brush with milk and cut slits in a design to permit escape of steam or prick well with fork. Bake in hot oven (425°F) 45 minutes, or until apples and crust are done.

**See page 168*

BAKED PIE SHELL

Prepare Victory Pie Crust as directed on page 168. Place dough on lightly floured board, shape round and pat flat with rolling pin. Then roll into 1½ -inch circle. Fold in half and place on bottom of inverted 9-inch pie plate. Open out folded half of pastry and fit snugly to plate. Trim off pastry to outer edge of plate and mark around rim with table fork dipped in flour. Prick crust well. Bake in hot oven (450°F) 15 to 18 minutes, or until lightly browned.

VICTORY PIE CRUST

1¼ cups sifted flour
½ teaspoon baking powder
½ teaspoon salt
3 or 4 tablespoons cold shortening
3 or 3½ tablespoons ice water*

Sift flour once, measure, add baking powder and salt, and sift again. Cut shortening into small pieces; add to flour and cut in until mixture is almost as fine as meal. Make small well in flour mixture. Turn 1 tablespoon ice water in this and mix quickly and lightly with surrounding flour only until a small ball of dough is formed. Do not over mix. Repeat this way, mixing all of the flour in separate portions. Then press portions together lightly but firmly into one dough ball. Makes enough pastry for 9-inch pie shell. Double recipe for pastry for two-crust pie.

Modern adaptation: If the crust should come out too dry and crumbly simply add small amounts of water until the mixture has a more doughy consistency.

* *Use only 3 tablespoons ice water with 4 tablespoons shortening; use 3½ tablespoons ice water with 3 tablespoons shortening.*

LEMON CHIFFON PIE

3 egg yolks, slightly beaten
1 cup water
½ cup sugar
1 package Lemon Jell-O
3 tablespoons lemon juice
1½ teaspoons grated lemon rind
dash of salt
3 egg whites
Baked Pie Shell (page 167 - 168)

Combine egg yolks and water in top of double boiler, mixing well. Add ¼ cup sugar and cook over hot water about 3 minutes, or until well heated, stirring constantly. Remove from fire. Add Jell-O and stir until dissolved. Add lemon juice and rind. Chill until slightly thickened. Add salt to egg whites and beat until foamy; then add remaining sugar gradually and continue beating until stiff. Fold slightly thickened Jell-O into egg whites. Pour into cold pie shell. Chill until firm.

CHEESE PIE

1 cup cottage cheese
½ cup milk
2 eggs, separated
¼ cup sugar
¼ teaspoon cinnamon
¼ teaspoon salt

Combine milk and cottage cheese and mash with a fork until fine and creamy. Add well beaten egg yolks, sugar, salt and cinnamon. Fold in egg whites. Pour into pastry lined pan. Bake for 10 minutes in a hot oven (425°F) and then lower heat to 350°F for 15 to 20 minutes, or until filling is firm and delicately brown.

To make pastry: Blend ½ cup margarine with 1½ cups flour sifted with ½ teaspoon salt. Add water for form stiff dough. Roll out on floured board to fit pan.

CHEESE AND APPLE PIE

1 recipe Victory Pie Crust (see page 168)
2 cups thinly sliced apples
¼ cup raisins or currants
½ cup sugar
½ teaspoon cinnamon
¼ teaspoon nutmeg
2 eggs, well beaten
½ cup light corn syrup
½ cup cottage cheese, strained
½ cups sour cream
1 teaspoon lemon rind

Roll out pastry about ¼-inch thick; line pie pan, flute edge. Combine apples, raisins, sugar, cinnamon, and nutmeg. Turn into unbaked pastry shell. Combine remaining ingredients and pour over apple mixture. Bake in hot oven (450°F) for 10 minutes; reduce heat to moderate (375°F) for 30 minutes and finish baking.

LEMON PUDDIN' PIE

1 tablespoon butter, softened
1 cup sugar
2 tablespoons enriched flour
3 egg yolks, unbeaten
1½ teaspoons grated lemon rind
1 cup milk
3 tablespoons lemon juice
3 egg whites, stiffly beaten
1 unbaked 9-inch pie shell

Cream butter and sugar; add flour, mix well. Add egg yolks, beat well (about 1 minute). Add rind. Add milk gradually. Add lemon juice. Fold in egg whites, beaten stiff but not dry. Turn into pie shell. Bake in hot oven (450ºF) for about 5 minutes; then reduce temperature to moderate (350ºF) and bake for about 30 minutes or until a knife inserted in the center comes out clean. Cool before serving.

Note: If desired, decrease sugar to ½ cup; add ¼ cup light corn syrup.

CANNED FRUIT PIE

1 double recipe Victory Pie Crust
3 to 4 tablespoons enriched flour
1/2 to 2/3 cup sugar
2 1/2 cups well-drained, canned fruit (cut in cubes)
3/4 cup fruit juice
1 tablespoons lemon juice
1 tablespoon butter

Roll out enough pastry for 1 crust at a time, keeping it about 1/8-inch thick. Line pie pan; trim edge.

Combine flour and sugar; add fruit. Toss about to mix thoroughly. Turn into pastry-lined pan. Add fruit juices; dot with butter. Moisten edge of under crust; adjust top crust; trim about ¼-inch beyond edge of pan. Tuck top crust under bottom crust; seal securely with pastry marker or fork. Make gashes in center of crust of allow escape of steam. Steam vents may be made in the form of a design. Bake in hot oven (450°F) for 10 minutes to set crust: reduce heat to moderate (375°F) for about 25 to 30 minutes to finish baking.

Note: Amount of flour and sugar depend upon juiciness and sweetness of fruit.

A lattice top may be used, if preferred.

Sugar-Saving Variation: Use ¼ to ½ cup sugar. Add ¼ cup corn syrup (light or dark). Decrease fruit juice to ½ cup.

FRESH FRUIT PIE

1 double recipe Victory Pie Crust (see page 168)
3 to 7 teaspoons enriched flour
1 to 1½ cups sugar
dash of salt
4 cups prepared fruit (cherries, grapes, peaches, rhubarb, plums, strawberries, raspberries, blackberries, blueberries, huckleberries, gooseberries)
1 tablespoon lemon juice (omit if fruit is tart)
2 tablespoons butter

Roll out about 2/3 or enough pastry for 1 crust at a time, keeping it about 1/8-inch thick. Line pie pan; trim edge. Combine flour, sugar, and salt; add to fruit. Toss about to mix thoroughly. Turn into pastry-lined pan. Sprinkle with lemon juice; dot with butter.

Moisten edge of under crust; adjust top crust; trim about ¼ inch beyond edge of pan. Tuck top crust under bottom crust; seal securely with a pastry marker or fork. Make gashes in center of crust to allow escape of steam. Bake in hot oven (450°F) for 10 minutes to set crust; reduce heat to moderate (350°F) for about 35 to 40 minutes to finish baking.

Note: Amount of sugar and flour depends upon sweetness, ripeness, and type of fruit used.

Sugar-Saving Variation: Use 4 to 7 tablespoons of enriched flour, ¼ to 1/3 cup sugar, 1/8 teaspoon salt, ½ cup light or dark corn syrup.

FRUIT HONEY COBBLERS

¼ cup honey
½ teaspoon cinnamon
2 teaspoons butter, melted
1 No. 2½ can peaches, drained, or 6 fresh peaches, pared and sliced

Combine honey, cinnamon, and butter. Add peaches. Place in individual baking dishes or custard cups. Use the following crust for topping:

1 cup sifted all purpose flour
1½ teaspoons baking powder, (or ¾ teaspoon double-acting)*
¼ teaspoon salt
2 teaspoons sugar
2 tablespoons shortening
2/3 cup milk

Sift flour once, measure, add baking powder, salt, and sugar; sift together twice. Cut in shortening until it resembles coarse meal. Add milk; stir until all flour is dampened. Drop dough on prepared fruit; spread evenly to edge. Bake in hot oven (425°F) for about 20 minutes, or until crust is nicely browned. Serve warm, with cream or hard sauce.

Note: Pitted cherries, apricot halves, or plums may be substituted for peaches.

Modern adaptation: A number 2½ can equals approximately 3½ cups. If using canned peaches two 15-ounce cans would be suitable for this recipe. Leftover peaches, if any, can be saved and used as a garnish. If custard cups are not available, this recipe can also be prepared in an 8 x 8-inch baking dish.

**Most modern baking powders are double-acting.*

War bonds poster. United States Government Printing Office. Circa 1942.

Other WW2 Home Front History — War Bonds

WW2 was a very costly endeavor. It was costly with the personal sacrifices that everyone had to make, it was also costly in money and the government needed extra help to pay for it. War Loan Drives soon began after the attack at Pearl Harbor and continued throughout the war. These promotional drives encouraged average citizens to buy war savings bonds. A savings bond is a loan made to the government that is paid back later, with interest. And it was everyone's patriotic duty at that time to buy bonds to help win the war. War bonds could be purchased at any time, however the war loan drives were an extra incentive.

Some Americans elected to have money taken out of their paychecks for bonds. Anyone with extra change could buy a war savings stamp to keep in a savings album. Once filled, the albums would be redeemed for a savings bond. Children could also by War Bonds. Their teachers were authorized to sell 10-cent war savings stamps one day each week. When their 10¢ war stamp albums were completed they would have $18.70 worth of savings stamps. They would then take their completed album, with a nickel, and redeem their $18.75 for a $25.00 savings bond. The bond would mature in 10 years and could then be cashed in.

"(The war bond drive) was outside the cafeteria at noontime. I can remember distinctly (actor) Cesar Romero. The girls were all sighing because he was such a handsome man in his navel uniform. At that time it was impressive, but not yet to the point I had idolized him or anything like that. I knew they were doing a good job, and it was selling war bonds. I bought a few, usually it was through payroll deductions."

— Margaret Mills, (Courtesy of the Arizona Historical Society, Central Arizona Division)

20 UNITED STATES OF AMERICA 20

OFFICE OF PRICE ADMINISTRATION

RATION COUPON

FOR

TWENTY

POINTS

MEAT, FATS, FISH, and CHEESES

20 OPA Form R-1615 ☆ 20

CHAPTER EIGHT

PUDDINGS AND OTHER DESSERTS

20 UNITED STATES OF AMERICA 20

OFFICE OF PRICE ADMINISTRATION

RATION COUPON

FOR

TWENTY

POINTS

PROCESSED FOODS

20 OPA Form R-1325 ☆ 20

Special ration recipes made it possible for those who enjoyed something sweet after a savory meal to have dessert without using too many ration points. These recipes used different ingredients, such as margarine, or sugar substitutes.

Most Americans today probably think of pudding as a thick, creamy dessert that comes from a little box of powdered mix. However the word "pudding" actually describes a number of foods with a soft, spongy, or creamy texture. Prepackaged pudding mixes, such as Jell-O, Royal and Knox, have been around since the late 19th and early 20th centuries, and all required cooking the product. Instant puddings, as we know them today, did not come on the scene until the 1950s. Puddings can also be made from scratch, and some today may argue that puddings made from scratch are healthier because they contain more natural ingredients and may not have the preservatives and other chemicals found in a pudding mix. Some of the pudding recipes that follow may require special equipment, such as double-boilers or a steamed pudding mold. These items can be found at kitchen specialty stores or on-line.

Short on Sugar?

The following table sets out sugar substitutes, the amount given being that required to equal 1 cup of refined sugar.

Maple sugar	*1 cup*
Maple syrup	*1 cup*
Honey	*1 cup*
Sorghum syrup	*1½ cups*
Cane syrup	*1½ cups*
Corn syrup	*2 cups*

—"*Ration-Time Recipes,*" The National Cotton Council of America, Memphis, Tennessee, circa 1942.

APPLE CRISP

1 quart sliced apples
¼ cup water
1¼ teaspoons cinnamon
¾ cup sugar
½ cup flour
½ cup margarine

Place the sliced apples in a shallow baking dish. Add the water and 1 teaspoon of cinnamon. Blend together the sugar, flour, and margarine until creamy in texture. Spread this mixture over the tops of the apples. Sprinkle with the remaining cinnamon. Bake uncovered in a moderately hot oven (400°F), 40 to 50 minutes, or until apples are tender and the top is brown.

CUSTARD

2 eggs, (or 4 egg yolks)
2 to 4 tablespoons sugar
¼ teaspoon salt
½ teaspoon flavoring
2 cups scalded milk*

Beat eggs or egg yolks. Add sugar, salt, flavoring and milk.

For Soft Custard: Cook over not-quite-boiling water, stirring constantly, just until coats spoon (20 minutes). Remove from heat, cool. Top with whipped cream, meringue, etc. Or serve over pudding, fresh fruit, etc.

For Baked Custard: Pour mixture into 6 custard cups or 8-inch casserole. Steam bake (set in shallow pan of water) 30 minutes in slow moderate oven (325°F).

**Pasteurization has taken the place of scalding. Heat milk, do not boil.*

OVEN-STEAMED PUDDING

1 1/2 cups sifted flour
2 teaspoons baking powder
1/2 teaspoon salt
1/3 cup sugar
2 tablespoons shortening
1 egg, beaten
2/3 cup milk
1 teaspoon vanilla

Sift flour once, measure, add baking powder, salt and sugar, and sift together three times. Cream shortening. Add sifted dry ingredients, egg, 1/3 cup milk and beat ½ minute longer. Turn into greased individual molds, filling ½ full. Cover tops with brown paper and tie securely. Place pan in 1 inch of hot water. Bake in moderate oven (375°F) about 55 minutes, or until done. Makes 6 servings.

Or turn into greased 1 ½-quart casserole, cover with paper, and tie securely. Bake in pan with water as directed about 1 hour.

Or turn batter into greased top of double boiler, cover with lid, and place over boiling water. Cook 1 hour or until done.

FRUIT RING PUDDING

2½ cups sifted enriched flour
3¾ teaspoons baking powder (or 1 ¾ teaspoons double acting)*
3 tablespoons sugar
¾ teaspoon salt
6 tablespoons shortening
¾ cup milk
1½ cups sour cherries, well-drained and chopped
2 tablespoons sugar

Sift flour once, measure, add baking powder, 3 tablespoons sugar, and salt; sift again. Cut in shortening with a pastry blender or two knives until mixture resembles coarse meal. Add milk; mix until all flour is dampened and mixture leaves sides of bowl. Roll into 14 x 8-inch rectangle. Spread dough with cherries and sprinkle with 2 tablespoons sugar. Roll up as for jelly roll. Cut into 10 pieces.

Place sections around outer edge of greased 9-inch layer cake pan to form circle. Pour the following sauce over the roll:

¼ cup sugar
3 tablespoons enriched flour
1/8 teaspoon salt
¾ cup fruit juice

Combine sugar, flour, and salt; add cherry juice gradually. Cook until thick. Pour sauce over roll. Bake in moderate oven (375°F) for about 1 hour or until done.

Note: If desired, decrease sugar to 2 tablespoons in sauce; add 2 tablespoons corn syrup. Peaches, apricots, pineapple, or canned berries may be substituted for cherries.

**Most modern baking powders are double-acting.*

FRUIT PUDDINGS

1½ cups sifted enriched flour
2¼ teaspoons baking powder (or 1½ teaspoons double-acting)*
¼ teaspoon salt
¼ cup shortening
¾ cup sugar
1 egg, unbeaten
¾ cup chopped figs, dates, currants, raisins, peaches or apricots
¾ cup milk
1 teaspoon vanilla or lemon extract

Sift flour once, measure; add baking powder and salt; sift together twice. Cream shortening; add sugar gradually, creaming well. Add egg, beat until light and fluffy. Add figs. Add dry ingredients alternately with milk and flavoring; mix well after each addition; beat well after last addition only. Turn into greased 1½ quart pudding mold, filling 2/3 full. Cover tightly. Steam about 1¼ hours for large mold, about 30 minutes for small molds. Serve at once with a lot of lemon sauce or cream.

Note: This pudding may be steamed in greased custard cups, if preferred. Fill cups 2/3 full; cover with double thickness of waxed paper; tie securely; steam as directed. Or pudding may be baked in an 8 x 8 x 2-inch pan in moderate oven (350°F) for 45 minutes or in greased custard cups for 35 minutes. If desired, decrease sugar to ½ cup; add ¼ cup corn syrup.

**Most modern baking powders are double-acting.*

APPLE PUDDING

2 cups sifted enriched flour
3 teaspoons baking powder (or 2 teaspoons double-acting)*
½ teaspoon salt
¼ cup shortening
¾ cup milk
2 tablespoons butter, softened
½ cup firmly packed brown sugar
1 teaspoon cinnamon
1 quart sliced apples
½ cup honey
few grains salt
2 tablespoons butter

Sift flour once, measure; add baking powder and salt, and sift together. Cut in shortening until quite fine; add milk all at once. Mix until all flour is dampened. Knead lightly for a few seconds to smooth dough. Pat or roll dough into a rectangle ¼-inch thick. Spread with softened butter. Sprinkle with combined brown sugar and cinnamon. Roll up as for jelly roll. Cut into 8 to 10 pieces.

Put apples in buttered 2-quart casserole or deep baking dish. Add honey and salt; dot with another 2 tablespoons butter. Place cut rolls on top of apples; bake in moderate oven (400°F) for about 30 minutes. Serve warm, with plain or sweetened whip cream.

**Most modern baking powders are double-acting.*

MERINGUE PUDDING

¼ margarine, melted
2 cups scalded milk*
2 cups soft bread crumbs
2 egg
3 tablespoons sugar
1 teaspoon allspice
1 tablespoon molasses

Cover bread with milk. Beat eggs, saving 1 white. Combine eggs, sugar, allspice molasses, and margarine. Add to bread. Bake in greased baking dish at 350ºF for 50 minutes. Whip remaining egg white into meringue. Cover pudding with meringue. Brown.

**Scalding milk was the process used before pasteurization.*

MOCK INDIAN PUDDING

2 cups milk
2 small eggs, well beaten
2 tablespoons molasses
3 tablespoons sugar
½ teaspoon cinnamon
¼ teaspoon ginger
2 cups Wheaties

Combine milk, eggs and molasses. Mix sugar, cinnamon, and ginger and add to milk mixture. Mix in Wheaties. Pour into greased 8-inch baking dish. Bake 1 to 1½ hours in slow moderate oven (325ºF). Serve warm with plain or whipped cream. Yield: 6 servings.

REFRIGERATOR BREAD PUDDING

1 envelope plain gelatin
2 cups milk
½ cup light or dark corn syrup or ⅓ cup sugar
¼ teaspoon salt
4 slices white bread (2½ cups cubed)
2 eggs, slightly beaten
1 teaspoon vanilla
nutmeg, if desired

Soften gelatin in ¼ cup cold milk. Scald remaining milk with corn syrup (or sugar) and salt in double boiler. Add gelatin and stir until dissolved. Remove crusts and cut slices of bread into cubes. Pour hot milk slowly over beaten eggs, stirring constantly. Return to double boiler. Add bread cubes and cook until custard consistency, stirring constantly. Remove from heat. Add vanilla and beat with rotary beater until frothy. Turn into one large (or individual molds) that have been rinsed in cold water first. Chill. When firm, un-mold and serve with cream or any sauce. Sprinkle with nutmeg.

Modern adaptation: Be careful not to boil the milk. The beaten eggs can be slowly added to the milk mixture in the double boiler, stirring constantly as directed in the original recipe, until they are well blended. To give the pudding a bolder flavor, add ¼ teaspoon ginger, ¼ teaspoon cinnamon, and ¼ nutmeg with the vanilla. The pudding can also be poured into ramekins and served with whipped cream, cinnamon, or nutmeg on top, as suggested in the original recipe.

FARINA SPEED PUDDING

1½ cups moist mincemeat
1 cup water
½ cup farina*
½ teaspoon salt
1 teaspoon grated lemon rind
½ teaspoon grated orange rind

Blend the mincemeat with water and bring to boil. Stir in farina and salt. Cook 3 minutes. Stir in lemon rind and orange rind. Serve with hot Hard Sauce.

Modern variation: Mincemeat may not be available outside of the holiday season. Applesauce or cranberry sauce may be used as a substitute, as can other pie fillings, such as apple, peach or raspberry. If using a fruit pie filling pureeing in a blender or food processor is recommended as well as omitting the salt. Serve with sprinkled sugar, or top with fruit or whipped cream.

**Farina is a cereal made from grains and other plant parts usually used in puddings. It is more commonly known as Cream of Wheat.*

HOLIDAY CRANBERRY PUDDING

1½ cups sifted flour
1 teaspoon baking powder
¼ teaspoon salt
2 cups raw cranberries
½ cup molasses
½ cup warm water
2 tablespoons shortening, melted
2 teaspoons baking soda

Sift together flour, baking powder and salt. Stir in raw cranberries. Mix and add molasses, warm water, melted shortening, and baking soda. Pour into greased 1-quart mold. Tie waxed paper loosely over top. Steam 2 hours. Unmold. Serve hot with Easy Vanilla Sauce or any desired sauce.

Easy Vanilla Sauce

¼ cup sugar
½ cup cream
¾ cup light corn syrup
2 tablespoons butter, melted
1 teaspoon vanilla

Mix sugar, cream and corn syrup. Heat but do not boil. Add melted butter and vanilla. Serve hot.

OLD-TIME RICE CUSTARD PUDDING

2 cups cooked rice
½ cup seedless raisins
2 cups scalded milk*
2 eggs, beaten
½ cup sugar
½ teaspoon salt
1 teaspoon vanilla
nutmeg

Mix rice and raisins. Place in 8-inch baking pan, 3 inches deep. Blend milk into beaten eggs, sugar, salt and vanilla. Pour over rice and raisin mixture. Sprinkle with nutmeg. Place pan in shallow pan of water. Steam bake 1½ hours in moderate oven (325°F). Serve warm or chilled, with or without cream.

**Pasteurization has taken the place of scalding.*

DELICIOUS COTTAGE PUDDING

2 cups sifted flour
2 teaspoons baking powder
½ teaspoon salt
3 tablespoons shortening
1 cup sugar
1 cup milk
½ teaspoon vanilla

Sift flour once, measure, add baking powder and salt, and sift again. Cream shortening, add sugar gradually, and cream together well. Add flour, alternately with milk, a small amount at a time, beating after each addition until smooth. Add vanilla. Bake in greased pan, 8 x 8 x 2 inches, in moderate oven (350°F) 50 to 60 minutes, or until done. Serve with hot Fruit-Jar Sauce (Below), or with chocolate sauce.

FRUIT-JAR SAUCE

2 tablespoons flour
3 tablespoons sugar
¼ teaspoon salt
1 cup syrup from canned fruit and water
bits of canned or fresh fruit
1 to 2 tablespoons lemon juice
½ teaspoon grated lemon or orange rind
dash of nutmeg

Mix flour, sugar and salt together in a small saucepan. Add fruit syrup gradually, stirring well. Boil gently 2 minutes, stirring constantly. Add fruit, lemon juice, rind, and nutmeg. Serve warm. Makes about 1¼ cups. (For a plain lemon sauce, omit fruit; increase lemon juice to 3 tablespoons.)

WHITE PLUM DUFF AND SAUCE

2 cups sifted flour
4 teaspoons baking powder
½ teaspoon salt
2 tablespoons sugar
2 tablespoons shortening
1 cup milk
2 cups cooked prunes (drained and pitted)

Sift together flour, baking powder, salt and sugar. Cut in shortening. Mix in milk. Spread open 4 large prunes on bottom of 1-quart greased mold. Cover with thin layer of batter, then layer prunes, etc., until all are used. Steam 1 hour. Serve hot with hot prune sauce.

Prune Sauce

3 tablespoons cornstarch
2/3 cups sugar
2 cups cold prune juice
3 tablespoons lemon juice or mild vinegar
1 tablespoon butter
½ teaspoon nutmeg

Mix ingredients together. Cook over low heat until thick, stirring often. Remove from heat. Add butter and nutmeg.

FRUIT WHIP

1 cup cut-up, pitted, well-drained, cooked fruit
3 to 5 tablespoons confectioners' sugar
dash of salt
1 teaspoon lemon juice
3 egg whites, stiffly beaten

Mix and chill cooked fruit, confectioners' sugar, salt and lemon juice. Fold in egg whites. Chill. May be served with sweetened whipped cream.

ORANGE CREAM

1 package lemon jelly powder*
1 cup hot water
½ cup sugar
1 cup orange juice
3 tablespoons grated orange rind
1 cup cream, whipped

Dissolve lemon jelly powder in hot water. Add sugar, orange juice and orange rind. Cool. Fold into whipped cream. Pour into 7-inch melon mold or 6 to 8 individual molds. Chill (about 2 hours). Un-mold. Garnish with fresh fruit. Makes 6 to 8 servings.

**Lemon Jell-O may be used as a substitute. Omit sugar.*

VANILLA ICE CREAM

1 cup scalded milk*
½ cup sugar
4 tablespoons flour
½ teaspoon salt
1 cup cream, whipped
1 teaspoon vanilla

Pour scalded milk into a mixture of sugar, flour and salt. Cook over hot water for 20 minutes (until slightly thick). Cool. Fold in whipped cream and vanilla. Freeze until firm, stirring occasionally. Serves 6.

Chocolate Ice Cream: Add 3 tablespoons cocoa to flour mixture.

Fruit Ice Cream: Add 1½ cups mashed fresh fruit pulp, sweetened to taste, to cooked mixture.

**Pasteurization has taken the place of scalding.*

Scrap drive poster. United States Government Printing Office. Circa 1942.

Other WW2 Home Front History — Scrap Drives

Virtually everyone could make a contribution to the war effort through scrap drives. Since all kinds of materials were needed to help win the war hardly anything was thrown away. Long before recycling, there were metal, rubber, and paper drives, and these scrap drives were a means for children in particular to help with the war effort. Schools participated in contests to meet city and state quotas for metal, rubber and paper. Some children would even donate their favorite toys to the various scrap drives. Toy production was also affected by the war. Certain types of toys, like steel wagons and skates and rubber squeak toys went out of production, with some toy makers substituting pine board for metal.

Rubber was like gold so families would save all their rubber bands, tying them up into balls and keeping for the next rubber drive. Tin foil from candy wrappers and cigarette boxes was also saved and rolled into little balls for metal drives. Old tools, metal buckets, tin cans, pots and pans and other pieces of scrap metal were reused. Lard or bacon grease that was no longer suitable for cooking would be taken to the butcher shop to be used for explosives.

"I remember the saving of rubber bands, tin foil and metal—that and more for this 'war effort.' There seemed to be a lot of patriotism and unity."

— Marge Hackett

20 UNITED STATES OF AMERICA 20
OFFICE OF PRICE ADMINISTRATION

RATION COUPON
FOR
TWENTY
POINTS
MEAT, FATS, FISH, and CHEESES

20 OPA Form R-1915 ☆ 20

CHAPTER NINE

CAKES AND COOKIES

20 UNITED STATES OF AMERICA 20
OFFICE OF PRICE ADMINISTRATION

RATION COUPON
FOR
TWENTY
POINTS
PROCESSED FOODS

20 OPA Form R-1325 ☆ 20

Wartime baking was particularly challenging. All of the essential ingredients needed for baking; flour, sugar, eggs, and shortening, were rationed. Un-rationed fats, such as chicken fat, home rendered lard, leftover pan drippings or a combination of half fat and half butter or margarine could be used as shortening substitutes.

Rendered fats were first cut away from meat or poultry, and then cut into smaller pieces. These pieces were then placed in a saucepan or double-boiler, melted over low heat, and then strained through several layers of cheesecloth. Once rendered they were placed in a tightly covered container and refrigerated.

Corn syrup, honey or molasses could be used in place of sugar. The recipes that follow also helped make precious ration points go further. Some omit eggs, while others use lower amounts of sugar or shortening.

Sugar rationing poster. Circa 1943.

OLD-FASHIONED JELLY ROLL

¾ cup flour
¾ teaspoon baking powder
¼ teaspoon salt
4 eggs, unbeaten
¾ cup sifted flour
1 teaspoon vanilla
1 cup tart red jelly

Sift flour once, measure. Combine baking powder, salt, and eggs in bowl. Place over smaller bowl of hot water and heat. With rotary egg beater, adding sugar gradually until mixture becomes thick and light-colored. Remove bowl from hot water. Fold in flour and vanilla. Turn into 15 x 10-inch greased pan, lined with paper to within ½-inch of edge, and again greased. Bake in hot oven (400°F) 13 minutes. Quickly cut off crisp edges of cake. Turn out on cloth covered with powdered sugar; remove paper. Spread with jelly and roll. Wrap in cloth and cool on rack.

EGGLESS UPSIDE DOWN CAKE

2 tablespoons butter or margarine
1/3 to 1/2 cup brown sugar, firmly packed
1 1/2 cups canned pineapple wedges, peach slices, or cooked prunes
1/2 cup broken pecan meats, if desired
1 recipe Delicious Cottage Pudding (page 190)

Melt butter in 8 x 8 x 2-inch pan or 8-inch skillet over low flame. Add brown sugar and cook and stir until thoroughly mixed. On this arrange fruit; sprinkle nuts over top.

Mix Delicious Cottage Pudding batter as directed and pour over contents of pan. Bake in moderate oven (350°F) 50 to 60 minutes, or until done. Loosen cake from sides of pan with spatula. Turn upside down on dish so fruit is on top.

EGGLESS CHOCOLATE CAKE

2 squares unsweetened chocolate
1 cup milk
1 3/4 cups sifted flour
3/4 teaspoon soda
3/4 teaspoon salt
1 cup sugar
1/3 cup shortening
1 teaspoon vanilla

Combine chocolate and milk in top of double boiler and cook over rapidly boiling water 5 minutes, stirring occasionally. Blend with rotary egg beater; cool.

Sift flour once, measure, add soda, salt, and sugar, and sift together three times. Cream shortening, add flour, vanilla, and chocolate mixture. Stir until all flour is dampened. Then beat vigorously 1 minute. Bake in two greased and lightly floured 8-inch layer pans in moderate oven (375°F) 20 minutes, or until done. Spread frosting between layers and on top of cake.

Cocoa Cake: Substitute 1/3 cup cocoa for chocolate. Sift it with the dry ingredients; add cold milk with vanilla.

EGGLESS WHITE CAKE

¼ cup shortening
1 cup sugar
2¼ cups sifted cake flour
or 2 cups sifted flour
½ teaspoon baking soda
½ teaspoon baking powder
1 teaspoon salt
1 cup buttermilk
1 teaspoon vanilla

Cream shortening with sugar. Sift together flour, baking soda, baking powder and salt. Add alternately with buttermilk. Blend in vanilla. Pour into greased and floured 8½-inch square pan. Bake 30 to 35 minutes in moderate oven (350ºF).

Eggless Spice Cake

In eggless white cake sift 1 teaspoon cinnamon, ½ teaspoon nutmeg, and ¼ teaspoon cloves with dry ingredients.

WARTIME CAKE

1 cup brown sugar
1 1/4 cups water
1/3 cup lard or other shortening
2 cups seeded raisins
½ teaspoon nutmeg
2 teaspoons cinnamon
1/2 teaspoon cloves
1 teaspoon salt
1 teaspoon baking soda
1 teaspoon and 2 tablespoons water
2 cups sifted flour
1 teaspoon baking powder

Mix brown sugar, 1¼ cups water, shortening, raisins, nutmeg, cinnamon, and cloves in saucepan. Boil for 3 minutes. Cool. Add salt, and baking soda dissolved in 2 tablespoons water. Blend in flour mixed with baking powder. Pour into greased, floured 8-inch square baking pan. Bake about 50 minutes in slow moderate oven (325°F). Delicious un-iced.

ONE EGG CAKE

1½ cups enriched flour
2¼ teaspoon baking powder, (or 1½ teaspoon double-acting)*
¼ teaspoon salt
¼ cup shortening
¾ cup sugar
1 egg, unbeaten
½ cup milk
1 teaspoon vanilla

Sift flour once, measure; add baking powder and salt; sift together three times. Cream shortening; add sugar gradually, creaming well. Add egg; beat until light and fluffy. Add dry ingredients alternately with milk and flavoring; mix well after each addition; beat well after last addition only. Bake in greased cake pans in moderate oven 350°F for one 8 x 8 x 2-inch loaf, for 45 minutes. 375°F for layers for 25 minutes. 375°F for cupcakes for 20 minutes.

Note: If desired, decrease sugar to ½ cup; add ¼ cup strained honey or corn syrup.

**Most modern baking powders are double-acting.*

TWO EGG CAKE

2 cups sifted enriched flour
3 teaspoons baking powder (or 2 teaspoons double-acting)*
½ teaspoon salt
½ cup shortening
1 cup sugar
2 eggs, well beaten
¾ cup milk
1 teaspoon vanilla

Sift flour once, measure; add baking powder and salt; sift three times. Cream shortening well. Add sugar gradually, creaming thoroughly. Add eggs; beat until mixture is light and fluffy. Add dry ingredients alternately with combined milk and flavoring; mix well after each addition; beat well after last addition only. Turn into greased, lined loaf, layer, or cupcake pans. Bake in moderate oven until done. 350ºF for 50 to 55 minutes for loaf. 375ºF for 25 minutes for layers, 20 minutes for cupcakes.

Variations

If desired, decrease sugar to ½ cup; add ½ cup strained honey. Decrease milk to ½ cup.

Decrease sugar to ½ cup; add ¼ cup light corn syrup. Use ¼ cup milk.

Decrease sugar to ¼ cup; add ¾ cup molasses. Decrease baking powder by 1 teaspoon. Add ½ teaspoon cloves, ¼ teaspoon nutmeg, and ¼ teaspoon to dry ingredients.

Combine 2 squares (2 oz) unsweetened chocolate, melted, 3 tablespoons hot water, 1½ tablespoons sugar, ¼ teaspoon soda, and 1½ tablespoons melted butter. Decrease milk to ½ cup. Add after the other dry ingredients in the basic recipe.

Add ½ cup chopped walnuts, ½ cup chopped raisins, figs, dates, or currant after adding the other dry ingredients in the basic recipe.

* *Most modern baking powders are double-acting.*

SILVER WHITE LAYER CAKE

2¼ cups cake flour
5 teaspoons baking powder (2 ½ teaspoons double-acting)*
1 teaspoon salt
1 ½ cups sugar
½ cup high-grade vegetable shortening (part butter adds flavor)
1 cup skimmed milk
1 teaspoon flavoring (vanilla, lemon or mint extract, etc.)
4 large egg whites, unbeaten

Sift together cake flour, baking powder, salt and sugar into bowl. Add shortening and ²/₃ cup skimmed milk. Mix with electric mixer on slow to medium speed (or beat with a spoon) for 2 minutes by clock. Scrape bowl frequently. Add remaining milk and unbeaten egg whites. Continue mixing 2 more minutes, scraping bowl frequently. Batter is thin. Pour into 2 well-greased and floured 8-inch round layer cake pans. Bake 30 to 35 minutes in moderate oven (350°F).

**Most modern baking powders are double-acting.*

GOLDEN LAYER CAKE

2¼ cups sifted cake flour
4 teaspoons baking powder (2 double-acting)*
1 teaspoon salt
1½ cups sugar
½ cup high-grade vegetable shortening (part butter adds flavor)
1 cup milk
1 teaspoon flavoring (vanilla, orange extract, etc.)
2 large eggs, unbeaten

Sift together cake flour, baking powder, salt and sugar into bowl. Add shortening and 2/3 cup milk. Mix with electric mixer on slow to medium speed (or beat with spoon) for 2 minutes by clock. Scrape bowl frequently. Add remaining milk, flavoring and eggs. Continue mixing 2 more minutes (scraping bowl frequently.) Batter is thin. Pour into 2 well-greased and floured 9-inch round layer cake pans. Bake about 30 minutes in moderate oven (350°F).

**Most modern baking powders are double-acting.*

CHOCOLATE DEVIL'S FOOD CAKE

$^{3}/_{4}$ cups cake flour
1$^{1}/_{4}$ teaspoon baking powder (or 1 teaspoon double-acting)
$^{1}/_{2}$ teaspoon baking soda
1 teaspoon salt
1$^{1}/_{2}$ cups sugar
$^{1}/^{2}$ cup high-grade vegetable shortening
$^{2}/_{3}$ cup milk (sweet, not sour)
2 large eggs, unbeaten
2 squares (2 ounces) unsweetened chocolate, melted

Sift cake flour, baking powder, baking soda, salt and sugar into bowl. Add shortening and $^{2}/_{3}$ cup milk. Mix with electric mixer on slow to medium speed (or beat with spoon) for 2 minutes by clock. Scrape bowl frequently. Add remaining milk and eggs. Mix one more minute, then add melted chocolate. Continue mixing 1 more minute (scraping frequently.) Pour into one greased and floured 8½-inch square layer cake pan or two 8-inch round pans. Bake in moderate oven (350°F) 45 to 50 minutes for square cake, or 30 to 35 minutes for layers.

**Most modern baking powders are double-acting.*

ORANGE LOAF CAKE

2 cups sifted cake flour
2 teaspoons baking powder (or 1½ to 1¾ double-acting)*
½ teaspoon salt
1¼ cups sugar
½ cup high-grade vegetable shortening (part butter adds flavor)
½ cup liquid (use grated rind and juice from 1 orange plus water to make ½ cup)
2 large eggs, unbeaten

Sift together cake flour, baking powder, salt and sugar in bowl. Add shortening and liquid. Mix with electric mixer (or beat with spoon) for 2 minutes by clock. Scrape bowl frequently. Add eggs. Continue mixing 2 more minutes (scraping bowl frequently.) Pour into greased and paper-lined 8¼-inch pan. Place on flat pan for more even baking. Bake 60 to 65 minutes in moderate oven (350°F). It may rise in center and crack. Delicious un-iced!

Modern adaptation: For a most zesty orange flavor omit water and use a ¼ cup of orange juice. Cake can be topped with powdered sugar, or sliced and served with fruit toppings, chocolate sauce or whipped cream.

**Most modern baking powders are double-acting.*

LORNA DOONE CAKE

1 cup quick oats
$1^1/2$ cups buttermilk
$^2/3$ cup margarine
1 cup brown sugar
2 eggs, separated
1 teaspoon lemon rind
2 cups sifted flour
1 teaspoon soda
1 teaspoon salt
$^1/4$ cup chopped nuts

Pour milk over oats. Cream sugar, margarine, yolks, add rind. Sift flour, soda, salt. Add nuts, creamed mixture and oats. Fold in whites, beaten stiff. Bake 350°F for 40 minutes.

CRUMB CAKE

2 cups flour
1 cup sugar
1 teaspoon each cloves, nutmeg and cinnamon
½ teaspoon salt
½ cup shortening
1 egg, beaten
2 tablespoons molasses
1 teaspoon baking soda
1 cup buttermilk

Sift together flour, sugar, cloves, nutmeg, cinnamon and salt. Cut in shortening very fine. Save half of crumb mixture for top of cake. To remainder mix in egg, molasses, and baking soda dissolved in buttermilk. Pour into greased and floured 8-inch square baking dish. Sprinkle reserved crumb mixture over top. Bake about 35 minutes in moderate oven (350°F).

HONEY SPICE CAKE

2 cups sifted flour
2 teaspoons baking powder
3/4 teaspoon salt
1 1/2 teaspoon allspice
1/2 cup shortening
1 teaspoon grated lemon rind
3/4 cup honey
2 egg yolks, unbeaten
1/2 cup milk
2/3 cups chopped raisins
1 teaspoon vanilla
2 egg whites
1/3 cup chopped walnut meats

Sift flour once, measure, add baking powder, salt, and allspice, and sift together three times. Cream shortening with lemon rind; add honey gradually, beating well after each addition. Add ¼ of flour and beat until smooth and well blended. Add egg yolks, one at a time, beating well after each. Add remaining flour in thirds, alternately with milk in halves, beating very well after each addition. Add raisins with last addition of flour. Add vanilla. Beat egg whites until stiff enough to hold up in moist peaks. Stir quickly but thoroughly into batter. Turn into greased 8 x 8 x 2-inch pan and sprinkle with nut meats. Bake in moderate oven (350°F) 55 minutes, or until done.

PEPPERMINT CANDY LAYER CAKE

1 cup sugar
½ cup margarine
½ teaspoon salt
2 eggs
2/3 cups milk
2 cups cake flour
2½ teaspoons baking powder

Cream together margarine, sugar and salt. Stir in beaten eggs. Sift flour with baking powder twice. Add flour mixture alternately with milk, about ½ of each at a time. Pour into two 8-inch layer pans, lined with paper or greased with margarine and floured. Bake at 375ºF for 35 minutes. When cool, put layers together with white icing. Decorate with peppermint candy using whole sticks on top, crushed on sides.

Modern adaptation: Since today's baking powders are double-acting decrease baking powder to 1¼ teaspoon. For best results use a small (6 cup) bundt pan, a medium (8 x 4 inch) loaf pan, or an 8 x 8-inch square pan. To add some peppermint flavor add ¾ teaspoon peppermint extract. If desired, top with Whipped Cream Topping, (page 219) using ½ cup crushed hard peppermint candy or 1/4 teaspoon peppermint extract.

FAVORITE MOLASSES CAKE

2¼ cups sifted flour
¾ teaspoon baking powder
½ teaspoon soda
¼ teaspoon salt
½ cup shortening
½ sugar
½ cup molasses
2 eggs, unbeaten
½ cup plus 1 tablespoon milk
1 teaspoon vanilla

Sift flour once, measure, add baking powder, soda, and salt, and sift together three times. Cream shortening, add sugar gradually, creaming thoroughly. Add molasses gradually and beat until light and fluffy. Add eggs, one at a time, beating well after each. Add flour, alternately with milk, a small amount at a time, beating after each addition until smooth. Add vanilla. Bake in greased 10 x 10 x 2-inch pan in moderate oven (350°F) 35 minutes, or until done. Spread with frosting.

EVERYDAY SPONGE CAKE

1 cup sifted flour
1 teaspoon baking powder
¼ teaspoon salt
2 eggs
1 cup sugar
1½ tablespoons butter or other shortening
6 tablespoons hot milk
1 teaspoon lemon juice
1 teaspoon vanilla

Sift flour once, measure, add baking powder and salt, and sift together three times. Beat eggs until very thick and light. Add sugar gradually, beating constantly. Quickly fold in half of flour; then fold in remaining flour. Melt butter and hot milk; add to batter, mixing quickly until smooth and well blended. Add lemon juice and vanilla. Turn at once into an 8 x 8 x 2-inch pan, which has been greased lightly, lined with waxed paper to within ½-inch of edge, and again greased lightly. Bake in moderate oven (350°F) 40 minutes, or until done. Sprinkle top of cake with powdered sugar, if desired.

SERVICE CAKE

$^{1}/_{3}$ cup shortening
$^{3}/_{4}$ cups sugar
2 eggs, well beaten
$1^{1}/_{2}$ cups sifted flour or $1^{2}/_{3}$ cups cake flour
$^{1}/_{2}$ teaspoon salt
$2^{1}/_{4}$ teaspoon baking powder (or $1^{3}/_{4}$ teaspoon double-acting)*
$^{1}/_{2}$ cup milk
1 teaspoon vanilla

Cream together shortening and sugar. Blend in well-beaten egg whites. Sift together flour and baking powder. Blend into creamed mixture alternately with milk and vanilla. Pour into greased and floured 8-inch square pan. Bake about 35 minutes in moderate oven (350°F).

* *Most modern baking powders are double-acting.*

SPICE CUP CAKES

$^{1}/_{3}$ cup margarine
1 cup brown sugar (packed tightly)
1 egg
1 teaspoon salt
$^{3}/_{4}$ cups sour milk or buttermilk
$1^{3}/_{4}$ cups flour
$^{3}/_{4}$ teaspoon baking soda
1 teaspoon cinnamon
$^{1}/_{4}$ teaspoon each cloves, nutmeg, ginger

Cream together margarine, sugar, and salt. Stir in beaten egg. Add sifted dry ingredients alternately with sour milk. Pour into margarine-greased cupcake pans and bake in a moderate oven (350°F) 20 to 25 minutes. Frost with any desired frosting. Decorate with candies.

RAISIN FRUIT CAKE

4 cups seeded raisins
2 tablespoons grated lemon rind or orange rind
1 tablespoon cinnamon
1 tablespoon allspice
2¼ cups water, or water and strong coffee
2½ cups nut meats
4 cups sifted flour
5 teaspoons baking powder
1½ cups sugar
½ cup shortening
2 eggs, well beaten
2 tablespoons vanilla

Combine raisins, rind, spices, and water in saucepan. Cover and cook gently for 8 minutes. Drain, pressing out as much liquid as possible. Measure liquid, add water or coffee to make 1½ cups, and reserve. Grind raisins with nuts.

Sift flour once, measure, add baking powder, salt, and sugar, sift together three times. Cream shortening very thoroughly, add flour mixture, eggs, vanilla, and reserved raisin liquid. Stir until all flour is dampened. Then beat vigorously 2 minutes. Add raisin-nut mixture and mix well. Turn into two 9 x 4 x 3-inch loaf pans which have been greased, lined with brown paper, and greased again. Sprinkle with chopped nut meats, if desired. Bake in moderate oven (350°F) 1 hour and 15 minutes, or until done. Let stand 5 minutes on cake rack; remove from pan, leaving paper attached. Cool. Wrap in cloth to store.

QUICK ORANGE FROSTING

1½ cups sifted confectioners' sugar
1½ teaspoons grated orange rind
2 tablespoons lemon juice
dash of salt
2 tablespoons hot melted butter or margarine

Combine sugar, orange rind, lemon juice, and salt. Add hot butter and beat vigorously 1 minute, adding more lemon juice, if necessary. Makes enough frosting to cover tops of two 8-inch layer, or top of 8 x 8 x 2-inch cake.

EASY FLUFFY FROSTING

1 egg white
dash of salt
½ cup light corn syrup or honey
1 teaspoon vanilla

Beat egg white with salt until stiff enough to hold up in peaks, but not dry. Pour syrup in fine stream over egg white, beating constantly 4 or 5 minutes, or until right consistency to spread. Add vanilla. Makes enough frosting to cover top of 10 x 10 x 2-inch cake, to tops and sides of two 8-inch layers.

COCOA MINUTE FROSTING

1 tablespoon butter or other shortening
3 tablespoons rich milk*
1½ cups sifted confectioners' sugar
4 tablespoons cocoa
dash of salt
½ teaspoon vanilla

Heat shortening with milk until it is melted. Mix together sugar, cocoa, and salt. Add hot milk, stirring to blend; then add vanilla and beat 1 minute. (If necessary, a little more milk may be added.) Makes enough frosting to cover tops of two 8-inch layers or 12 large cup cakes.

**Before pasteurization, rich milk was the layer under the heavy cream layer and the lighter milk below. Half and half is a good substitute.*

FLUFFY FROSTING

1 cup dark corn syrup
2 egg whites
¼ teaspoon vanilla

Pour corn syrup and egg whites in the top of a double boiler; beat vigorously over boiling water until very light and thick. Remove from heat, add the vanilla, and beat occasionally until cool and thick enough to spread between the layer and on the top and sides.

BROILED HONEY ICING

2 tablespoons butter
3 tablespoons honey
1 tablespoon top milk*
½ cup coconut
dash of salt

Mix ingredients together. Spread on warm cake. Broil slowly until icing bubbles and browns, but does not burn.

**Before pasteurization, top milk was the layer of cream that floated to the top. Substitute Half and Half or condensed milk.*

HONEY ICING

1 cup honey
2 egg whites, stiffly beaten

Heat honey to boiling. Boil one minute until honey thins somewhat. Pour in stiffly beaten egg whites and beat until fluffy and holds shape.

VICTORY ICING

¾ cup light corn syrup
2 egg whites, stiffly beaten
½ teaspoon lemon extract
½ teaspoon orange extract
pinch of salt

Heat corn syrup to boiling. Pour in stiffly beaten egg whites, beat until fluffy. Blend in lemon and orange extracts and a pinch of salt.

JELLY ICING

1 cup red jelly
2 egg whites, stiffly beaten

Gradually beat jelly into egg whites. Beat until smooth and stands in peaks. Red vegetable coloring may be added.

DOUBLE-BOILER SYRUP ICING

¼ cup sugar
½ cup syrup
1 egg white

Mix all ingredients in top of a double-boiler. Place over boiling water. Beat with rotary beater until thick. (About 5 minutes.)

DRIED FRUIT ICING

¾ cup (1/4 lb) dates
¾ cup (1/4 lb) figs or raisins
1 cup nuts (1/4 lb)
3 tablespoons lemon juice
hot water

Grind and mix fruits and nuts. Mix with lemon juice. Add hot water, enough to spread thin.

RAISIN TOPPING

1 cup raisins, ground
1/2 cup water
1/8 teaspoon salt
1/2 teaspoon cinnamon
dash of cloves

Mix ingredients in saucepan. Cook and stir until thick. (About 5 minutes.) Cool slightly. Spread on warm cake.

WHIPPED CREAM TOPPING

1 cup whipping cream
½ cup crushed peppermint candy
or ½ cup crushed peanut brittle
or 4 tablespoons jam or marmalade

Whip whipping cream until stiff. Fold in crushed candy or jam or marmalade.

MERINGUE TOPPING

1 egg white, stiffly beaten
½ cup confectioners' sugar
1 teaspoon flavoring (vanilla, lemon extract, etc.)
2 tablespoons butter, softened (optional)

Beat egg white until stiff. Gradually add in confectioners' sugar and flavoring. For richer icing add softened butter. Spread on baked cake.

PEANUT BARS

1 cup sifted enriched flour
1 1/2 teaspoons baking powder (or 1 teaspoon double-acting)*
1/2 teaspoon salt
1/3 cup shortening
1 cup firmly packed brown sugar
2 eggs, well beaten
2/3 cup chopped peanuts
1/4 cup milk
1 teaspoon vanilla

Sift flour once, measure; add baking powder and salt; sift together twice.

Cream shortening; add sugar gradually, beating until light. Add eggs; mix well. Add peanuts and combined milk and flavoring. Add dry ingredients in two portions; mix well. Turn into well-greased 12 x 9 x 2-inch loaf pan. Bake in moderate oven (350°F) for about 20 minutes. Cool in pan before making into bars or squares.

**Most modern baking powders are double-acting.*

LEMON-FROSTED FRUIT BARS

1 egg yolk
¼ cup brown sugar, packed in cup
¼ cup molasses
½ cup sour cream
1½ cups sifted flour
¼ teaspoon baking soda
½ teaspoon baking powder
¼ teaspoon salt
½ teaspoon ginger
½ cup nuts, chopped
½ cup cut-up pitted dates
½ cup confectioners' sugar
lemon extract

Mix egg yolk, brown sugar and molasses. Blend in sour cream. Sift together flour, baking soda, baking powder, salt and ginger. Blend into first mixture. Stir in nuts and dates. Spread into greased 8x12-inch pan. Bake about 15 minutes in moderately hot oven (400°F). Cut into 48 bars (1x2-inch). Cool in pan. Frost with confectioners' sugar beaten into egg white. Add pinch of salt and lemon extract. (To taste.)

GINGEROONS

3 1/4 cups sifted enriched flour
3 teaspoons baking powder (or 2 1/2 teaspoons double-acting)*
1 teaspoon baking soda
1 teaspoon salt
1 teaspoon cinnamon
1 teaspoon ginger
1/2 cup shortening
1 cup sugar
2 eggs, unbeaten
2/3 cup dark molasses

Sift flour once, measure; add baking powder, baking soda, salt, and spices; sift together three times.

Cream shortening; add sugar gradually, beating until light. Add eggs, one at a time; beat about one minute after each addition. Add molasses; beat well. Add dry ingredients in 3 portions; mix well. Drop by spoonfuls onto greased baking sheets. Sprinkle lightly with sugar. Bake in hot over (400°F) for about 10 to 12 minutes until done. Do not stack or store until cold. Makes about 3½ dozen cookies.

Modern adaptation: Dark corn syrup may be used as a substitute for molasses.

**Most modern baking powders are double-acting.*

DROP FRUIT COOKIES

1½ cups sifted enriched flour
1½ teaspoons baking powder (or ¾ teaspoon double-acting)*
½ teaspoon salt
½ teaspoon allspice
½ teaspoon cinnamon
½ cup shortening
1 cup sugar
1 egg, unbeaten
¾ cup chopped figs, dates, raisins, currants, etc.
½ cup chopped nutmeats
1 teaspoon vanilla
⅓ cup milk

Sift flour once, measure; add baking powder, salt and spices, sift again.

Cream shortening; add sugar gradually, creaming well. Add egg; beat thoroughly. Add fruit, nutmeats, and flavoring. Add dry ingredients alternately with milk; stir until thoroughly mixed. Drop by teaspoonfuls onto greased baking sheet allowing room for spreading. Bake in hot oven (425°F) for about 10 to 12 minutes until done. Do not stack or store until cold. Makes about 3 dozen cookies.

* *Most modern baking powders are double-acting.*

CARROT HONEY COOKIES

2 cups sifted enriched flour
2 teaspoons baking powder (or 1 teaspoon double-acting)*
¼ teaspoon baking soda
½ teaspoon salt
½ teaspoon cinnamon
½ teaspoon nutmeg
2 cups rolled oats
1 cup chopped raisins
1 cup chopped walnuts or nut meats
½ cup shortening
1 cup strained honey
2 eggs, well beaten
1 cup grated raw carrots

Sift flour once, measure; add baking powder, baking soda, salt and spices; sift twice. Add oatmeal, raisins, and nut meats; mix well.

Cream shortening; add honey, creaming thoroughly. Add eggs, mix well. Add carrots. Add dry ingredients in 2 or 3 portions, mixing well. Drop by spoonfuls onto greased baking sheet. Flatten out with a floured fork. Bake in moderate oven (350ºF) for about 20 to 25 minutes until done. Do not stack or store until cold.

**Most modern baking powders are double-acting.*

MONKEY-FACED COOKIES

½ cup plus 2 tablespoons shortening
1 cup brown sugar
2½ cups flour
1 teaspoon baking soda
½ teaspoon each of salt, ginger, and cinnamon
½ cup molasses
½ cup rich sour milk*
1 teaspoon vinegar
raisins

Cream shortening with brown sugar. Sift together flour, baking soda, salt, ginger and cinnamon. Mix molasses with sour milk. Mix alternately with flour mixture. Blend in vinegar. Drop by teaspoon on greased baking sheet. Place 3 raisins or bits of citron on each for eyes and mouth. Bake 10 to 15 minutes in moderate oven (350°F). Yield: about 3 dozen cookies.

**Buttermilk can be used as a substitute.*

BUTTERSCOTCH SQUARES

¼ cup margarine
1 cup brown sugar
¼ teaspoon salt
1 egg
1 cup sifted flour
1 teaspoon baking powder
1 teaspoon vanilla
¼ cup pecan meats

Cream together margarine, sugar, and salt. Blend in beaten egg. Add flour and baking powder sifted together. Then add nut meats and vanilla and spread the mixture in a lightly greased shallow pan (about 9-inch square). Bake in moderate oven (350°F) 25 to 30 minutes. While hot, cut into strips about an inch wide and three inches long.

PEANUT BUTTER COOKIES

¾ cup margarine
¾ cup granulated sugar
2 tablespoons peanut butter
1 egg, well beaten
2 cups all-purpose or bread flour
1 teaspoon baking powder
1 teaspoon vanilla extract

Cream margarine and sugar together until light and fluffy. Add peanut butter and egg. Blend thoroughly. Sift flour and baking powder together three times. Add vanilla and dry ingredients to creamed mixture. Mix well. Put through a cookie press. Bake cookies on a cookie sheet that has been well-greased with margarine. Bake in moderate oven (350°F) until done – approximately 10 minutes. Yield – 108 cookies.

PECAN DELIGHTS

1/2 cup margarine
2/3 cup brown sugar
1 egg yolk
1 cup flour
1/8 teaspoon cream of tarter
1/2 cup chopped pecans
pecan halves

Cream the margarine and sugar together. Add the egg yolk and mix well. Add the dry ingredients which have been sifted together. Add the chopped pecans. Form teaspoons of the dough into balls and place on baking sheets. Top each cookie with a pecan half, and bake in a very moderate oven (325°F) 12 to 15 minutes. Remove immediately from the baking sheets. Yield: 1½ dozen.

FROSTED CREAMS

1/3 cup margarine
1/3 cup sugar
1/2 teaspoon salt
1/3 cup molasses
1 egg
1 1/2 cups flour
1/4 teaspoon ginger
1/2 teaspoon soda

Cream together margarine, sugar, and salt. Add molasses and beaten eggs. Sift flour with soda, salt and ginger and stir into mixture. Place on cookie sheet and roll to ½-inch thickness. Bake in a moderate oven (350°F). While still warm cut into strips. Frost with powdered sugar made into a thin paste by the addition of milk or water.

DOUBLE-DECKER COOKIES

1/2 cup margarine
1/2 cup sugar
1/3 teaspoon salt
1 egg yolk
½ teaspoon vanilla
1½ cups flour
1 teaspoon baking powder
3 tablespoons milk
2 tablespoons cocoa

Cream together margarine, sugar, and salt. Blend in egg and vanilla. Sift flour and baking powder and add alternately with milk. Divide dough in half. Work cocoa into one part. Roll each out to a thin sheet. Cut with cookie cutter into desired shapes. Bake in moderate oven (350°F) 10 minutes. Put two cookies together with paste made by moistening confectioners sugar with milk or cream.

SOFT MOLASSES COOKIES

3 cups sifted cake flour
1½ teaspoons baking soda
½ teaspoon salt
1 teaspoon ginger
1½ teaspoons cinnamon
½ cup shortening
1 cup sugar
1 egg, unbeaten
½ cup shortening
1 cup sugar
1 egg, unbeaten
½ cup molasses
1 cup sour milk or buttermilk
½ teaspoon vanilla

Sift flour once, measure, add baking soda, salt, and spices, and sift together three times. Cream shortening, add sugar gradually, creaming until light and fluffy. Add egg and beat well; then add molasses. Add flour, alternately with milk, mixing well after each addition. Add vanilla. Chill 1 to 2 hours, or until firm enough to hold shape. Drop from teaspoon on lightly greased baking sheet, placing about 2 inches apart. Bake in hot oven (400ºF) 13 to 15 minutes, or until done. Makes 6 dozen cookies.

FIG SURPRISES

3½ cups sifted flour
3 teaspoons baking powder
½ teaspoon salt
½ cup shortening
½ cup brown sugar, firmly packed
1 egg, well beaten
1 teaspoon vanilla
⅓ cup milk
Fig Filling (below)

Sift flour once, measure, add baking powder and salt, and sift again. Cream shortening, add sugar gradually, creaming until light and fluffy. Add egg and vanilla, then add flour, alternately with milk, mixing well after each addition. Chill until firm enough to roll.

Roll ⅛-inch thick on lightly floured board. Cut with floured 2½-inch cutter. Put 1 rounded teaspoon Fig Filling on a circle. Place another circle on top, and press edges together. Bake on ungreased baking sheet in hot oven (425°F) 8 minutes, or until done. Makes 2 dozen cookies. (Strawberry jam, fig jam, or any desired preservatives may be used for filling in cookies.)

Fig Filling: Mix together 1½ cups ground figs, ⅓ cup sugar, and ⅔ cup boiling water. Cook 5 minutes, or until thick, stirring constantly. Remove from fire. Add 1 to 2 tablespoons lemon juice. Cool. Raisins may be substituted for figs; use ½ cup water.

PARTY SUGAR COOKIES

2 cups sifted cake flour
1 teaspoon baking flour
1/2 teaspoon salt
1/2 teaspoon cinnamon
1/4 teaspoon nutmeg
2/3 cup sugar
1/3 cup shortening
3 tablespoons milk
2 egg yolks, unbeaten
1/2 teaspoon lemon extract

Sift flour once, measure, add baking powder, salt, and spices, sift again. Measure sugar into bowl. Heat shortening with milk until all shortening is melted. Add immediately to sugar and beat ½ minute. Add egg yolks; beat ½ minute longer. Add lemon extract and half of flour mixture and beat until blended. Then add remaining flour, 1/3 at a time, beating until smooth. Cover with waxed paper and chill several hours, or until firm enough to roll.

Roll dough 1/8-inch thick on a lightly floured board. Cut with floured cutters in assorted shapes. Place on lightly greased baking sheet; sprinkle with sugar. Bake in hot oven (400°F) 7 minutes, or until done. Cool. Christmas-shaped cookies may be decorated and tied with bright ribbons to hang on Christmas tree. Makes about 2½ dozen cookies.

War Jobs Rcruiting Poster. United States Government Printing Office. Circa 1943.

Other WW2 Home Front History — Women Working in the Defense Industry

For the first time in history, women left the home, en masse, to work in factories performing jobs that had once only been done by men. So many men had joined the service that women were needed to replace them in all kinds of production work. Women helped build tanks, ships, and airplanes. These complex pieces of machinery were built on assembly lines and companies like Consolidated Aircraft built different components in different parts of the county, shipping them off to other plants for final assembly. This was done so that in the event of an enemy attack the loss of one factory would not shut down the entire line of production.

While newsreels of the day may have made it look glamorous, it was, in reality, very tedious and sometimes dangerous work. However, the women working these plants often found friendship and moral support from other women they were working with. Just about all of them had a husband, a fiancé, a son, or a brother overseas fighting, while they stayed behind and fought "The War Back Home." It stands to reason that some of those friendships would have lasted a lifetime.

"I heard that they were wanting workers at Goodyear, so in 1943 I applied for a job. I helped to make trailing edges for the B-24 plane. Practically all of the men had gone off to the service, so most of the men (at Goodyear) were either old or weren't qualified to be in the service. There were about 18 women and 3 men in our section."

— Laura Harris, (courtesy of the Arizona Historical Society, Central Arizona Division)

BIBLIOGRAPHY

"Best Foods Menu Planner War Rationing and Nutrition.. Pamphlet. Best Foods, Inc. 1943.

"Commemorating the End of Shoe Rationing." Le Roux, Gerry. Internet Article. sciencelens.co.nz/2012/10/30/end-of-shoe-rationing/. Downloaded Spring, 2016.

"The Food Timeline." www.foodtimeline.org.

"The Effects of Rationing in World War II", Oke, Heather, http://www.batavia.k12.il.us/pps/HistWeb/text/96prjcts/ww2bat/reports/hmfront/ration/hoke1.htm. Downloaded Spring, 2001.

"Fightin' Food, Fifth Edition" Foods Education Department, Pillsbury Flour Mills Company. Pamphlet. U.S. Government's National Nutrition Program, 1943.

"Gelatin A Valuable Supplementary Protein Food A 'Fighting Food" for Wartime Nutrition", Knox Gelatin Company. Pamphlet circa 1943. Publisher and publication date unknown.

Gifford, Marie. *69 Ration Recipes for MEAT.* Armour and Company. Chicago, circa 1942. Publication date unknown.

"Goodyear Builds Tools of Victory", Shadegg, Stephen C., Arizona Highways, Volume 19, No. 5, May, 1943, pp 15-19; 41-42.

How to bake by the Ration Book. G.F. Corp. 1943. U.S.A.

Interviews. w/Steve Hoza, WWII Historian, Arizona Historical Society, Central Arizona Division, by Gayle Martin, 2000-2001.

"Kodak created, U.S. Government adopts "V-Mail"... for communication with our men on distant fronts" Full page magazine advertisement, Eastman Kodak Company, Rochester, N.Y., circa 1942.

Melton, Brad and Smith, Dean, editors. *Arizona Goes to War The Home Front and Front Lines During World War II.* Tucson, Arizona: The University of Arizona Press, 2003.

National Cotton Council of America. Ration•Time RECIPES. National Cotton Council of America, Memphis, Tennessee, circa 1942. Publication date unknown.

"The three "Rs" of WARTIME BAKING RATIONS 'RICHMENT AND RECIPES", Ames, Mary Ellis, Directors, Pillsbury's Cooking Services. Pamphlet, circa 1943. Publisher and publication date unknown.

"Why Canned Fruits, Vegetables, And Soups Are Rationed." Government Pamphlet, U.S. Office of Price Administration, January, 1943.

"Your Share: How to prepare appetizing, healthful meals with foods available today." Pamphlet. Betty Crocker Home Service Staff, General Mills, Inc., Minneapolis, Minnesota, 1943.

ABOUT THE AUTHOR

Gayle Martin has had a lifelong interest in history and the arts. A second-generation native of Phoenix, Arizona, Gayle graduated from Arizona State University and later attended the Academy of Art College in San Francisco. She worked for a number of years as a graphic designer, winning numerous awards, including Denver Advertising Federation's Unsung Heroine of the Year.

Gayle's life changed dramatically when she returned to Arizona and began working with the Arizona Historical Society Museum in Tempe as a docent tour leader. She later became a member of the museum's living history program. Her composite character, Anna Ferguson, World War II Housewife and Defense Worker, told the story of the home front. For six years, she inspired children and adults alike with her character's ability to face challenges with dignity during uncertain times. In 2005, she published her first book, *Anna's Kitchen, a Compilation of WWII Recipes You Can Create in Your Own Kitchen,* as a spin-off from her living history presentations. After Anna's Kitchen, Gayle wrote the award-winning Luke and Jenny series of children's books about the history of the American west.

Gayle currently resides in Tucson, Arizona, where she founded a publishing company, Good Oak Press, LLC., in 2011. She now writes romance novels as Marina Martindale, and in her spare time she enjoys traveling, photography, and music.

For more information about Gayle's books please visit her website at www.qgoodoakpress.com.

Recipe Index

A

B

C

D

E

F

G

H

J

K

L

M

N

V

W

Z

www.ingramcontent.com/pod-product-compliance
Lightning Source LLC
Chambersburg PA
CBHW021346150726
47989CB00005B/2128

* 9 7 9 8 2 1 5 4 3 0 7 3 6 *